The Rosenberg Espionage Case

by Francis Moss

FAMOUS
TRIALS

Lucent Books, San Diego, CA

Titles in the Famous Trials series include:

The Boston Massacre
Brown v. Board of Education
Cherokee Nation v. Georgia
The Dred Scott Decision
The Impeachment of Bill
  Clinton
Miranda v. Arizona
The Nuremberg Trials

The O.J. Simpson Trial
Roe v. Wade
The Salem Witch Trials
The Scopes Trial
The Trial of Adolf Eichmann
The Trial of Joan of Arc
The Trial of John Brown
The Trial of Socrates

Library of Congress Cataloging-in-Publication Data

Moss, Francis.
   The Rosenberg espionage case / by Francis Moss.
     p. cm. — (Famous trials)
   Includes bibliographical references and index.
   Summary: Discusses the famous espionage trial of Julius and Ethel Rosenberg, covering both the prosecution and defense, the government's pursuit of this couple, and the aftermath of the trial.
   ISBN 1-56006-578-8 (lib. : alk. paper)
   1. Rosenberg, Julius, 1918–1953—Trials, litigation, etc. Juvenile literature. 2. Rosenberg, Ethel, 1915–1953—Trials, litigation, etc. Juvenile literature. 3. Trials (Espionage)— United States Juvenile literature. 4. Spies—United States— Juvenile literature. [1. Rosenberg, Julius, 1918–1953—Trials, litigation, etc. 2. Rosenberg, Ethel, 1915–1953—Trials, litigation, etc. 3. Spies. 4. Trials (Espionage)] I. Title. II. Series.
KF224.R598M67   2000
345.73'0231—dc21   99-31389
                                                              CIP

Copyright © 2000 by Lucent Books, Inc.
P.O. Box 289011
San Diego, CA 92198-9011
Printed in the U.S.A.

Table of Contents

Foreword

"The law is not an end in and of itself, nor does it provide ends. It is preeminently a means to serve what we think is right."

William J. Brennan Jr.

THE CONCEPT OF JUSTICE AND THE RULE OF LAW are hallmarks of Western civilization, manifested perhaps most visibly in widely famous and dramatic court trials. These trials include such important and memorable personages as the ancient Greek philosopher Socrates, who was accused and convicted of corrupting the minds of his society's youth in 399 B.C.; the French maiden and military leader Joan of Arc, accused and convicted of heresy against the church in 1431; to former football star O.J. Simpson, acquitted of double murder in 1995. These and other well-known and controversial trials constitute the most public, and therefore most familiar, demonstrations of a Western legal tradition that dates back through the ages. Although no one is certain when the first law code appeared or when the first formal court trials were held, Babylonian ruler Hammurabi introduced the first known law code in about 1760 B.C. It remains unclear how this code was administered, and no records of specific trials have survived. What is clear, however, is that humans have always sought to govern behavior and define actions in terms of law.

Almost all societies have made laws and prosecuted people for going against those laws, but the question of which behaviors to sanction and which to censure has always been controversial and remains in flux. Some, such as Roman orator and legislator Cicero, argue that laws are simply applications of universal standards. Cicero believed that humanity would agree on what constituted illegal behavior and that human laws were a mere extension of natural laws. "True law is right reason in agreement with nature," he wrote,

4

world wide in scope, unchanging, everlasting. . . . We may not oppose or alter that law, we cannot abolish it, we cannot be freed from its obligations by any legislature. . . .This [natural] law does not differ for Rome and for Athens, for the present and for the future. . . . It is and will be valid for all nations and all times.

Cicero's rather optimistic view has been contradicted throughout history, however. For every law made to preserve harmony and set universal standards of behavior, another has been born of fear, prejudice, greed, desire for power, and a host of other motives. History is replete with individuals defying and fighting to change such laws—and even to topple governments that dictate such laws. Abolitionists fought against slavery, civil rights leaders fought for equal rights, millions throughout the world have fought for independence—these constitute a minimum of reasons for which people have sought to overturn laws that they believed to be wrong or unjust. In opposition to Cicero, then, many others, such as eighteenth-century English poet and philosopher William Godwin, believe humans must be constantly vigilant against bad laws. As Godwin said in 1793:

Laws we sometimes call the wisdom of our ancestors. But this is a strange imposition. It was as frequently the dictate of their passion, of timidity, jealousy, a monopolizing spirit, and a lust of power that knew no bounds. Are we not obliged perpetually to renew and remodel this misnamed wisdom of our ancestors? To correct it by a detection of their ignorance, and a censure of their intolerance?

Lucent Books' *Famous Trials* series showcases trials that exemplify both society's praiseworthy condemnation of universally unacceptable behavior, and its misguided persecution of individuals based on fear and ignorance, as well as trials that leave open the question of whether justice has been done. Each volume begins by setting the scene and providing a historical context to show how society's mores influence the trial process and the verdict.

Each book goes on to present a detailed and lively account of the trial, including liberal use of primary source material such as direct testimony, lawyers' summations, and contemporary and modern commentary. In addition, sidebars throughout the text create a broader context by presenting illuminating details about important points of law, information on key personalities, and important distinctions related to civil, federal, and criminal procedures. Thus, all of the primary and secondary source material included in both the text and the sidebars demonstrates to readers the sources and methods historians use to derive information and conclusions about such events.

Lastly, each *Famous Trials* volume includes one or more of the following comprehensive tools that motivate readers to pursue further reading and research. A timeline allows readers to see the scope of the trial at a glance, annotated bibliographies provide both sources for further research and a thorough list of works consulted, a glossary helps students with unfamiliar words and concepts, and a comprehensive index permits quick scanning of the book as a whole.

The insight of Oliver Wendell Holmes Jr., distinguished Supreme Court justice, exemplifies the theme of the *Famous Trials* series. Taken from *The Common Law*, published in 1881, Holmes remarked: "The life of the law has not been logic, it has been experience." That "experience" consists mainly in how laws are applied in society and challenged in the courts, a process resulting in differing outcomes from one generation to the next. Thus, the *Famous Trials* series encourages readers to examine trials within a broader historical and social context.

Introduction

America in the Depression

I N THE 1930s, THE United States experienced the worst economic downturn in its history, known now as the Great Depression. Businesses and factories failed, putting 30 million people out of work. Banks foreclosed on farms because farmers were unable to make payments on their loans, driving families off land they had owned for generations. All over the country, thousands of men, women, and children lost their homes and were forced to live in shantytowns or in temporary encampments.

During the economic failure of the 1930s, known as the Great Depression, whole families found themselves forced to live in shantytowns.

Some Americans who called themselves "Progressives," "Socialists," or "Communists" believed that the U.S. economic system was to blame for the depression. These people argued that the rich—whom they called the "ruling class"—were responsible for this economic disaster and that they were profiting from it while the ordinary workers continued to suffer. Some American workers, seeing the wealthy dressed in furs and finery, motoring to nightclubs or sailing to Europe on luxurious ocean liners, began to agree with this view. Many loyal Americans began to think that other social and political systems might provide better lives for working people. The country most often held up as a model of fairness for the working class was the Soviet Union, where the ruling Communist Party imposed an economic system that eliminated private ownership of property. Wealthy and even middle-class Americans, however, were terrified by the idea of communism, which they saw as a threat to their beliefs in individual liberty and the sanctity of private property.

With millions homeless and out of work because of the depression, and many more threatened with the loss of their jobs, the American Communist Party was able to gain thousands of new members. Many other Americans who never joined the party sympathized with its aim, which was the creation of a truly equal and classless society. In an effort to recruit new members, Communist Party members joined labor unions and spoke on college campuses.

America in World War II

With the onset of the Second World War, the United States found itself in an uneasy partnership with the Soviet Union, an alliance necessary to defeat the Axis powers—Germany, Italy, and Japan. Despite the fact that both the United States and Russia were fighting a mutual enemy, there was never a strong trust between the two countries. The Soviets believed that the United States wanted to achieve dominance in the world; the United States attributed similar ambitions to the Soviets. The Soviets' fears were not eased when the United States exploded

President Harry Truman (center), Winston Churchill of England (left), and Joseph Stalin of Russia (right) sit at a World War II conference. America and the Soviet Union kept a tenuous alliance during the war, but cooperation quickly turned to competition with the beginning of the Cold War.

atomic bombs over the Japanese cities of Hiroshima and Nagasaki.

At the war's end, the thin veneer of cooperation between the two countries disappeared. In particular, the Soviets worried that the United States, by possessing the atomic bomb, had the means necessary to dominate the world. At the same time, the U.S. government felt threatened by the rapid spread of communism from the Soviet Union to its neighbors in Eastern Europe.

The Beginning of the Cold War

The United States watched helplessly as one by one, Poland, Czechoslovakia, Hungary, Bulgaria, and Romania fell under Communist influence. The U.S. fears grew even more intense when in 1949 China fell to the Communists and, in 1950, Communist North Korea invaded South Korea.

By the early 1950s, everywhere Americans looked, it seemed, communism was at work, tightening its grip on nations in Europe and in Asia. As one nation after another came to be

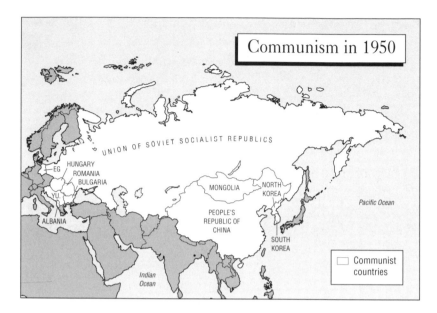

Communism in 1950

UNION OF SOVIET SOCIALIST REPUBLICS

HUNGARY
EG
ROMANIA
BULGARIA
YU.
ALBANIA

MONGOLIA

NORTH KOREA

PEOPLE'S REPUBLIC OF CHINA

SOUTH KOREA

Pacific Ocean

Indian Ocean

☐ Communist countries

ruled by local Communists, fear of communism outside America's borders became fear of communism within. Increasing numbers of Americans began to believe that the United States was in danger from Communists on its very own soil.

Before long, anti-Communist sentiment reached hysteria. People imagined Communists everywhere. For example, in 1950, in a Chinese restaurant in Houston, Texas, a woman radio producer asked the restaurant owner for help in producing a program about China. A diner overheard the conversation and called the police, informing them that people were "talking communism." The woman and her companion were arrested and held for fourteen hours, until the police realized their error.

Efforts to combat what some characterized as "the Communist menace" sometimes became extreme. In Pasadena, California, a three-year-old girl was hired to model for an art class at a tax-sponsored college. Her mother was told that the child could not be paid unless she signed an oath of loyalty to the United States.

With scarcely a breather from World War II, the United States and the Soviet Union confronted each other in a "cold war." Each side made efforts to learn the intentions and strategies of the other, through the use of spies and informants. The Soviets were anxious to learn the secrets of the weapon the Americans had used to defeat Japan; the Americans were just as determined to keep that information secret. Of the many individuals who were accused of spying for the Soviets, none were more famous or controversial than Julius and Ethel Rosenberg.

The Rosenbergs: Spies or Martyrs?

By all outward appearances, Julius and Ethel Rosenberg were a pleasant, even dowdy, middle-class couple in their late thirties. They were both short, with round faces and dark hair. Julius's slightly owlish look was enhanced by his rimless glasses. Ethel had the kindly yet worried expression seen on almost every good mother. They had two young children, Robert and Michael. The Rosenbergs went for walks in their Brooklyn, New York, neighborhood on Sunday afternoons. By their very ordinariness, the Rosenbergs were perfectly suited for espionage.

But were Julius and Ethel Rosenberg really spies? The U.S. government, which arrested, tried, and convicted them, said "Yes." Millions of Americans and others said (often loudly) "No." To some, the Rosenbergs were traitors to their country. To others, they were innocent victims of a nation caught in the grip of anti-Communist hysteria.

The Rosenberg case is one of the most controversial events in U.S. history. No other trial has engendered as much debate, has aroused such passion, has generated as many articles, books, and television shows as the Rosenberg matter has. Every element of the case has been subjected to the most intense scrutiny. The Rosenbergs' arrest, their incarceration while awaiting trial, the trial itself, the involvement of the Communist Party, and accusations that anti-Semitism played a role in the trial have all been a part of the Rosenberg saga.

In the decades since the trial, books and articles have attempted to prove the Rosenbergs' innocence and to demonstrate the flimsiness of the government's case. Other books and articles claim to prove their guilt. Both opinions have been argued, with more or less equal eloquence and conviction, until

Protesters outside the White House carry signs demanding execution for the Rosenbergs. The couple was accused of giving secrets regarding the atomic bomb to the Soviets, but their guilt or innocence is still a matter of controversy.

recent times. But perhaps the real significance today of the Rosenbergs and their trial is the picture of the times in which they lived and died, of the paranoia and hysteria that the mere mention of communism could cause.

Chapter 1

The Pursuit of the Rosenbergs

IN 1945, GENERAL LESLIE Groves, a senior military official who oversaw the development of America's atom bomb, confidently predicted that it would be at least ten years before the Soviet Union could develop its own atomic weapon. Just four years later, however, in August 1949, the Soviets exploded their first atomic bomb.

U.S. military and government leaders were convinced that the Soviets could not have developed their own A-bomb so quickly without the help of spies within the American scientific community. In addition, other world events added to the U.S. government's unease: In April 1949 the Chinese Communists, led by Mao Tse-tung, had taken control of China. In June 1950, Korea, a country that had been divided into two countries following World War II, erupted into war when the Communist-led North invaded the South.

Suddenly the postwar world no longer seemed safe to many Americans. Germany and Japan had been defeated, but international communism had risen to take their place in the imaginations of many people. Some government leaders argued that if communism was a threat to the rest of the world, it could be a threat to the United States as well.

The Trail to the Rosenbergs

In June 1950, the FBI received its first leads concerning a spy ring operating in the United States, a ring that was delivering

13

closely guarded information about America's most powerful weapon, the atomic bomb, to the Soviet Union.

The trail leading to the American spy ring began in England in 1949. The British Intelligence Service, MI-6, had been questioning a German-born British scientist, Klaus Fuchs, who had worked on the construction of the first atomic bomb during World War II. Fuchs had been suspected of being a possible Communist spy when the U.S. Central Intelligence Agency decoded some intercepted Soviet shortwave radio transmissions. Among those uncovered was a progress report on America's effort to create an atom bomb, known as the Manhattan Project, that Fuchs had sent to Russia.

A British intelligence investigator sent to question Fuchs was stunned when the scientist willingly admitted that while working on the atomic bomb in Los Alamos, New Mexico, he had handed over highly classified data to a spy working for the Soviets.

Fuchs never revealed his motive in confessing, but Ronald Radosh and Joyce Milton, in their book *The Rosenberg File*, reveal that Fuchs had become disillusioned with the Soviets after learning of their brutal treatment of people in the countries of Eastern Europe following World War II. In addition, Fuchs told

Pictured is German scientist Klaus Fuchs, who sent top secret information regarding the atomic bomb to the Soviets through an American contact known to him only by the code name "Raymond."

his British interrogators that he had a means of compartmental-
izing information in his mind that allowed him to separate his
scientific work from his espionage work.

Fuchs revealed to his MI-6 interrogators that his main contact in the United States had been an American whose code
name was "Raymond." Fuchs's first meeting with Raymond was
the stuff of spy novels. As Fuchs described it, "I was to meet an
individual who would be wearing gloves and carrying another
pair of gloves in his hand. I would be carrying a ball."[1]

When this news of Fuchs's confession reached the United
States, FBI investigators, alarmed at this serious breach of atomic
security, immediately went through their files and determined
that "Raymond" was probably a man named Harry Gold, who fit
Fuchs's vague description of his contact as being "About forty . . .
heavyset . . . with a receding hairline."[2] But Fuchs was madden-
ingly unwilling or unable to positively identify Harry Gold from
the blurry pictures that the FBI sent to the agents of MI-6.

In New York, Gold was already under FBI surveillance, having been previously identified as a courier for the Communists.
While the FBI was making its case against him, Gold read about
Fuchs's arrest in the New York papers and panicked. When, a
few days later, FBI agents Richard Brennan and Scott Miller
questioned Gold for the third time, he confessed: "I am the man
to whom Klaus Fuchs gave the information on atomic energy."[3]

J. Edgar Hoover, famed director of the FBI, was pleased
with Gold's confession. But he needed more information. He
made it clear to the agents in charge that Gold was to be
"exhaustively interviewed for descriptions of his contacts in the
espionage field,"[4] especially those contacts he had made with
people working at the A-bomb test site in Los Alamos, New
Mexico.

Under further questioning, Gold told the FBI that, in 1945,
his Soviet contact, Anatoli Yakovlev, had instructed him to go to
Albuquerque, New Mexico, to meet with a soldier who had
information to give him. Gold did as he was told, and the soldier
handed over classified information concerning the layout of the
base at Los Alamos.

Harry Gold (center) was the American contact through whom the Soviets received information from the atomic testing facilities at Los Alamos, New Mexico.

Gold thought the soldier's name was either Frank Kessler or Frank Martin. But he remembered the soldier's wife's name as Ruth. From Gold's description of the soldier and his wife, the FBI identified David and Ruth Greenglass. On June 15, 1950, the FBI called David Greenglass in for questioning.

In 1945, at the time of his meetings with Gold, David Greenglass was a machinist at the Los Alamos A-bomb facility. He and his wife, Ruth, had been members of the Communist Party since they were teenagers. Both were passionate and idealistic believers in socialism as a cure for the world's economic and social problems. David's older sister, Ethel, was also a party member and an enthusiastic supporter of the Soviet Union, as was her husband, Julius Rosenberg.

Meet the Rosenbergs

Julius Rosenberg was born on May 12, 1918, in New York City, the son of Polish immigrants Harry and Sophie Rosenberg. Despite his father's wishes that he study to become a rabbi,

HOW THE FBI FOUND DAVID GREENGLASS

The FBI's identification of David Greenglass as Harry Gold's contact was an accident. In 1950 Greenglass was one of a group of soldiers questioned in a routine investigation concerning atomic workers who had stolen small amounts of uranium as souvenirs. When the FBI saw Greenglass's name on a list of those who had been interviewed about the uranium thefts and saw that he had a wife named Ruth and had lived in the area Gold identified as the place he visited in Albuquerque, that was enough to prompt agents to show Gold a photograph of Greenglass. Even so, Gold was hesitant, only tentatively identifying the pictures. However, when the FBI provided photos of the Greenglasses' residence, Gold recognized the house as the one he had visited. With this evidence in hand, the FBI brought Greenglass in.

David Greenglass, a machinist working at the Los Alamos atomic testing facility, matched the description of the man who gave maps of the facility to Harry Gold.

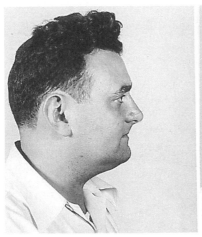

Julius pursued his primary interests of science and politics. Enrolling in City College of New York, Julius studied electrical engineering, a course of study that made him eligible to join the Federation of Architects, Engineers, Chemists, and Technicians (FAECT), a militant union with a pro-Communist leadership. The union often leafleted nonunion factories and machine shops in an effort to recruit new members among employees. About this time, Julius also joined the Steinmetz Club, the campus branch of the Young Communist League.

Julius Rosenberg was well regarded by others in FAECT for his passionate and logical debates on the political and social issues of the day. Politics so interested Julius that by the time he met his wife-to-be, Ethel Greenglass, he was spending more time on political activities than on his studies. At Ethel's urging, however, Rosenberg became less politically active for a while, and he was able to graduate in 1939, one semester behind the rest of his class.

Julius and Ethel Rosenberg wearing swim attire. They met in the 1930s while he was a student at City College of New York.

Ethel Greenglass Rosenberg was born on September 28, 1915, in New York City to Barnet and Tessie Greenglass. The Greenglass family was poor, which might have led Ethel, who was a strong-willed and intelligent woman, to her enthusiasm for the causes of working people. Ethel Greenglass displayed an early inclination to fight on behalf of other workers. In her first job, for example, as a clerk in a shipping company, she was fired for leading 150 of her coworkers in a sit-down strike. Ethel showed her resolve by filing a complaint about her firing with the National Labor Relations Board. She won her case, and then immediately found another, and better-paying, job.

Ethel Greenglass also was interested in politics, joining the Young Communist League and eventually the Communist Party. In addition to her clerk's job, Ethel enjoyed singing, alone as well as with a choir. In fact, Ethel was waiting to go on stage to sing at a New Year's Eve benefit when she first met Julius Rosenberg. The couple was married not long afterward, in the summer of 1939. They later had two children, Robert and Michael, who in 1950 were three and seven years old.

After leaving college, Julius worked at odd jobs until the fall of 1940, when he was hired as a civilian employee of the U.S. Army Signal Corps. Julius was promoted in 1942 to the position of inspector, and the new position, with its higher pay, allowed the Rosenbergs to move to a new three-bedroom apartment.

Around this same time, Julius and Ethel became full members in the American Communist Party. Julius was the chairman of branch 16B of the party's industrial division, which met at the Rosenbergs' apartment. David and Ruth Greenglass were members of the same branch, and, when David got his assignment to Los Alamos in 1943, Julius began to ask him for information about operations at the atomic facility.

The Rosenbergs' close affiliation with the Communist Party did not last, however. In 1944, during a reorganization of the party, Julius and Ethel failed to renew their membership. When Ruth Greenglass was questioned on this point by FBI investigators, she claimed that the Rosenbergs dropped out in order to spy for the Russians. Some say that it was common practice for a would-be spy to drop out before beginning espionage activities. Max Gordon, a former editor for the U.S. Communist newspaper *The Daily Worker*, has said that "by and large, anyone who became a spy for the Soviet Union was completely separated from the Party."[5] While no concrete evidence supports the idea that the Rosenbergs dropped out in order to become spies, the fact that they did so is cited as evidence of their guilt. However, a more innocent explanation might be that Julius had also just begun working for the army's Signal Corps and his Communist Party membership would have endangered his job.

Whatever his reasons for leaving the Communist Party, doing so did not save Rosenberg's job. Early in 1945, Rosenberg was fired from the Signal Corps after an army intelligence investigation revealed his past membership in the Communist Party. In 1946 Rosenberg started a machine shop business with his brother-in-law and father-in-law, David and Barnet Greenglass. None of the men was a good businessman, however, and the firm lost money, causing bad feelings between the Greenglasses and the Rosenbergs.

David was a more easygoing type and able to forgive his brother-in-law, but Ruth Greenglass was embittered by the loss of the business. She also felt that Julius's never-ending demands on her husband to deliver sensitive information about his work at Los Alamos endangered both her and David. What was worse, Julius seemed indifferent to their peril. The Rosenberg defense would later argue that it was this estrangement that made it easier for the Greenglasses to act as witnesses against David's sister and their brother-in-law. When questioned years later, however, both Ruth and David denied it.

There were other pressures on David. In February 1950, just four months before he was first called in for questioning by the FBI, David's wife had been badly burned in a home fire and was under a doctor's care. In addition, she was in the middle of a fragile pregnancy, having had a miscarriage a few years before.

With the FBI breathing down his neck, David Greenglass foresaw a bleak future: either a life on the run with a sick and unhappy wife or a life in jail, away from all he knew. Seeing his life unraveling before his eyes, David took the path of least resistance. He told the FBI interrogators everything about his espionage activities on behalf of the Soviet Union.

Greenglass revealed to the FBI that he was the "Frank Kessler" Harry Gold had mentioned in his confession. He then went on to give details on his activities. Greenglass described how, in June 1945, when he and Ruth visited the Rosenbergs, Julius cut the front of a Jell-O box into two irregularly shaped pieces. One David would keep, the other would be given to him by the contact, who would then receive the espionage data Greenglass had prepared for him.

Greenglass further confessed that it was Harry Gold, who had arrived in Albuquerque with the other half of the Jell-O box and that he had handed over to Gold the plans for the Los

A February 1955 view of the entrance to the Los Alamos atomic testing facility.

Alamos base. Later, Greenglass told the FBI agents interrogating him that he had made drawings of a critical part of the atomic bomb, called a "lens mold," and sketches of the inner workings of the bomb that was later dropped on Nagasaki. Greenglass told investigators that he had given those drawings to his brother-in-law, Julius Rosenberg, and, at his questioners' urging, he re-created drawings of the lens mold from memory. These drawings would later become critical to the prosecution's case, and a subject of controversy then and in years since.

The FBI Tightens the Noose

FBI agents wasted no time in pursuing David Greenglass's lead regarding Julius Rosenberg's involvement in espionage. But they did not immediately realize how central Rosenberg was to what the newspapers would later call the "atom spy ring." In

THE MOST IMPORTANT QUESTION

Why would someone betray their country by committing espionage? To most people, the very idea is abhorrent. Even today, with the fear and mistrust of the Cold War fading into history, it is hard to imagine the circumstances under which one might give vital secrets to agents for another nation. Yet many Americans gave information to the Soviets, for a variety of reasons. For some at least, the reasons were rooted in idealism.

The Rosenbergs and many others like them hated the Nazis and sympathized with the bravery of the Russian people who were battling them. As Julius Rosenberg's Soviet handler, Aleksandr Feklisov, said in an interview published in the *Washington Post*, "It was not difficult to find people to help us. I had the impression that if we put an advertisement in the paper with a request for information, thousands of people would have replied."

In addition, the idealists saw the Great Depression as an event signaling the downfall of the capitalist system, and they looked to Soviet communism as a solution to society's ills. Morton Sobell, who was convicted along with the Rosenbergs and served eighteen years in prison, wrote of the depression in his book, *On Doing Time:* "Remember, this was a time when there was 30 percent unemployment and people were getting thrown onto the street every day. . . . People like me were attracted to communism because it seemed to offer a rational explanation for what was wrong with society."

June 1950, when the FBI began intensive surveillance of the Rosenbergs, Julius was regarded as just a single link in a chain that might lead the FBI to the center of the conspiracy.

But Rosenberg proved to be a tough adversary. When Special Agents John A. Harrington and William Norton came to his Knickerbocker Village apartment on New York City's Lower East Side on June 16, 1950, Rosenberg refused to admit them, but he did agree to accompany them to their offices in Foley Square for questioning. Julius reacted calmly when informed that his brother-in-law had been held in custody for several days. But he grew angry when Agent Harrington asked, "What would you say if we told you your brother-in-law said you asked him to supply information to the Russians?"

"Bring him here. I'll call him a liar to his face,"[6] Rosenberg replied.

At that time, the FBI did not have sufficient grounds to charge Rosenberg with any crime, so they were forced to let him go. But they still needed to keep the pressure on David Greenglass, to force him to testify against his brother-in-law. And they needed to get results soon: If Julius Rosenberg was the spy he appeared to be, the agents reasoned, then he would most certainly flee the country.

After he was released by the FBI, Julius Rosenberg sought legal help. He went to the offices of Victor Rabinowitz, the legal counsel for FAECT who had helped Julius before when he had been dismissed by the Signal Corps. But Rabinowitz turned Rosenberg down. He had defended other accused spies and did not want to be involved with yet another case of this kind.

Rabinowitz sent Rosenberg to another attorney noted for his defense of left-wing and radical clients, Emmanuel "Manny" Bloch. Bloch had already made a name for himself in other political cases for both the National Lawyers Guild and the Civil Rights Congress, two organizations the FBI had identified as either "Communist front" or "Communist-dominated" groups. He agreed at once to take Julius Rosenberg as a client.

The case at this point revealed some strains between two powerful government agencies. FBI director Hoover was in a

Emmanuel "Manny" Bloch, who had defended a number of radicals and left wing clients, took the Rosenberg case in 1950 after the FBI questioned Julius Rosenberg about his involvement in atomic espionage.

hurry to put some high-profile Communists on trial, but the Justice Department, more concerned with building the strongest case possible, was (in the FBI's view at least) dragging its feet. In an attempt to generate more evidence, the FBI brought Ruth Greenglass in for questioning in early July 1950.

Although Ruth had assured Julius and Ethel that she and David intended to resist the government's pressure, under interrogation at the Foley Square FBI offices she confirmed her husband's testimony: Julius Rosenberg, with Ethel Rosenberg in the room, had asked David to spy and had given him the cut-up Jell-O box cover. She also identified Harry Gold as the man who had appeared at their apartment in Albuquerque.

The FBI now had the information necessary to proceed. The Justice Department agreed, and on Monday evening, July 17, 1950, a warrant was issued for the arrest of Julius Rosenberg.

The Arrest of Julius and Ethel Rosenberg

At 7:30 P.M. that same Monday, FBI agents Harrington and Norton arrived at the Rosenberg apartment, arrested Julius, and handcuffed him in front of his frightened wife and children. He was taken first to Foley Square for arraignment on charges of conspiracy to commit espionage. Bail was set at $100,000. Rosenberg was then put in jail at Manhattan's Federal Detention Center, called "the Tombs."

Ever since the confession of Klaus Fuchs had made front-page headlines in the United States, journalists had been looking for more on the story. Reporters for several newspapers, sensing a break in the "spy ring" saga, hurried to question Julius Rosenberg. But he continued to maintain his innocence to the press.

Up until her husband's arrest, Ethel Rosenberg had not been under suspicion, even though the Greenglasses' statements had placed Ethel in the room where espionage was being discussed. But as Julius Rosenberg continued to claim his innocence, the FBI began to consider accusing Ethel as a means of exerting pressure on her husband. J. Edgar Hoover sent a message to the Justice Department:

> There is no question that if Julius Rosenberg would furnish details of his extensive espionage activities it would be possible to proceed against other individuals . . . [and] *proceeding against his wife might serve as a lever in this matter.*[1]

J. Edgar Hoover, director of the FBI, ordered that pressure be put on Ethel Rosenberg in order to make Julius, who still adamantly maintained his innocence, implicate others in atomic espionage.

The grand jury impaneled to consider the Rosenberg espionage case was not at first interested in indicting Ethel, even after her first appearance before them on August 8, 1950, when she refused to answer most questions about her Communist affiliations. Three days later, Ethel Rosenberg made a return appearance before the grand jury, at which time she was asked—and again refused to answer—most of the same questions put to her in her first appearance. Then, in a move that surprised almost everyone, Ethel Rosenberg was arrested as she left the grand jury room. So hasty was the arrest, Ethel was not even given time to arrange for care for her children. They were initially placed in a Brooklyn children's shelter and later taken in by their grandmother, Tessie Greenglass. Ethel Rosenberg then hired Manny Bloch's father, Alexander Bloch, a competent trial lawyer—but one inexperienced in political trials—to represent her.

The Government Indictment

The Rosenbergs, along with Ruth and David Greenglass, were charged with conspiracy to commit espionage under the U.S. Espionage Act of 1917, Subsection (a) of Section 32. In addition, Anatoli Yakovlev, the Rosenbergs' alleged Soviet handler (who had left the country in 1946), was named as a co-conspirator.

The indictment specifically charged that the defendants

THE CONSPIRACY STATUTES

The legal requirements to prove conspiracy are so vague that the conspiracy law has been called both the "prosecutors' friend" and "the last resort of the people." Hearsay testimony is admissible, and once prosecutors prove the existence of a conspiracy, they can make each conspirator liable for the acts of any of the others, whether or not he or she knew of them. Finally, the conspiracy does not need to have been successful for charges to be brought.

Supporters of the Rosenbergs have argued that the government chose to charge the couple under the conspiracy statutes rather than charging them with espionage because the government had no proof that the Rosenbergs had ever spied or had encouraged others to spy. Although the government did have evidence of actual espionage, revealing it might have also forced the prosecution to reveal its sources.

"did conspire, combine, confederate and agree, with intent and reason to believe that it would be used to the advantage of a foreign nation, to wit, the Union of Soviet Socialist Republics, to communicate, deliver and transmit . . . documents, writings, sketches, notes, and information relating to the National Defense of the United States of America."[8] The indictment went on to allege twelve overt acts committed by Ruth and David Greenglass and Ethel and Julius Rosenberg. Not one of the acts cited in the indictment was itself a crime; the acts consisted of such things as Julius giving Ruth Greenglass money, Julius and Ethel conferring with David and Ruth, and David Greenglass traveling to New Mexico. It would be the job of the prosecution to show how these acts were part of the conspiracy to commit espionage.

Chapter 2

The Prelude to Trial

THE U.S. GOVERNMENT HAD Julius Rosenberg, Ethel Rosenberg, and David Greenglass in custody. But now it needed to make a case—by uncovering other members of the spy ring and by demonstrating just how far their activities extended. Spurring on FBI and Justice Department investigators was their embarrassment over revelations coming from England concerning Klaus Fuchs, who had given valuable information on the atom bomb to the Soviets and whose confession had led the FBI to "Raymond." In addition, the American public's mood of anti-Communist hysteria and fear of the Soviet Union further motivated both FBI investigators and U.S. attorneys.

The investigators knew that Ethel Rosenberg was suffering by being forcibly kept from her beloved husband and children. They hoped to use her vulnerable state as leverage in their efforts to get her husband, Julius, to confess. Reports from the Women's House of Detention adjacent to the

Pictured in this 1953 photo are Michael and Robert Rosenberg, the sons of Julius and Ethel Rosenberg.

Tombs, where she was being held, indicated that each day during yard exercise, Ethel would go to the fence and press against it, hoping to see her husband. The FBI, following Hoover's idea, promised Ethel a quick release from prison and a reunion with her children if she would testify against her husband. But she refused to admit to any crime, nor would she betray her husband.

Applying what became known as the "lever strategy" (from Hoover's memo) on both ends, the FBI also let Julius Rosenberg know about his wife's suffering; he too refused to bend. But the FBI had more than one strategy to pursue. While the Rosenbergs sat in prison, investigators followed up leads that would expose other members of the "atom spy ring."

Spies Escape

From David Greenglass's confession, the FBI had gathered information that implicated some of Julius Rosenberg's friends in the spy ring. Some of the names investigators turned up were already in FBI files as suspected spies or Communist sympathizers.

One of these friends was Joel Barr. U.S. intelligence agencies had seen Barr's name in decoded messages from the KGB, the Soviet State Security Committee, written in 1948. They also knew he was a friend of Julius Rosenberg's from their days as students at City College of New York. But the FBI did not connect Barr with espionage activities until Greenglass alleged that Rosenberg had told him that Barr was a member of the spy ring.

At that point, the FBI made efforts to locate Barr, who was in Paris. On July 25, an attaché at the U.S. Embassy in Paris went to Barr's apartment, but he had vanished. No one had seen him since June 16—the same day that David Greenglass's arrest was announced in the press. Joel Barr was never seen again.

Another object of the FBI's interest was Al Sarant, another friend of Julius Rosenberg's. He came under FBI investigation because he was Joel Barr's best friend and former business partner. In the 1940s Sarant had opened a business with Joel Barr called Sarant Laboratories, and he had tried to get navy contracts for developing new methods of voice transmission. The FBI was curious about other contacts Sarant and Barr might have had

An alleged spy for the Russians, Joel Barr, who was a friend of Julius Rosenberg, vanished following the arrest of David Greenglass and was never seen again.

but—at that time still confident that they could find Barr—they did not push Sarant very hard and released him while keeping him under surveillance.

While visiting his sister on Long Island, Sarant and a female friend eluded their FBI tail and fled to Mexico. Like Barr, Sarant and his companion vanished from sight forever.

Yet another friend of Rosenberg's from high school, Max Elitcher, became key to the government's investigation. Elitcher had first come to the attention of the FBI in 1948, when government cryptographers decoded a 1944 message from Moscow to its consulate in New York in which Elitcher's name was mentioned. The FBI engaged in some routine surveillance of Elitcher during the summer of 1948 but saw nothing incriminating in his behavior.

Elitcher's name arose again in July 1950, after Julius and Ethel Rosenberg were arrested and another of Rosenberg's old friends, Morton Sobell—at that time Elitcher's next door neighbor—fled the country. The FBI came to Elitcher's home to question him, and Elitcher told the agents that according to Rosenberg, Sobell was spying for the Soviets.

Under intensive questioning during July and August 1950, Elitcher admitted belonging to the Communist Party and that, because of his job at the U.S. Navy Ordnance Bureau, he had been approached several times by Julius Rosenberg and asked to gather information useful to the Soviets. But Elitcher swore he never engaged in espionage.

A Suspect Caught

The same day that Joel Barr left all his belongings in Paris and vanished, Morton Sobell, an engineer employed at Reeves Instrument Company, had asked his boss for a leave of absence, claiming he was exhausted and overworked. Although Sobell was working on an important project, he was granted a leave.

Leaving mail and milk deliveries piling up on his front porch, Sobell flew to Mexico with his wife, Helen, their young son, and his step-daughter. But his flight was poorly planned and unsuccessful. Sobell later claimed that he took his family to Mexico because he feared persecution for his left-wing beliefs, not because he feared arrest as a spy. Nevertheless, Sobell was seen at the Mexican ports of Vera Cruz and Tampico in a panic,

Another friend of Rosenberg, Morton Sobell, was captured by the FBI in Mexico.

trying to book passage for himself and his family to Europe. He failed because neither he nor his family had valid passports, having come to Mexico on tourist cards.

Sobell eventually left Mexico, but not for a destination he wanted. On August 16, 1950, Sobell and his family were abducted by armed men, taken to the U.S. border, and the next day were turned over to the FBI. He was indicted along with the Rosenbergs.

The Government Prepares for Trial

By the end of February 1951, more than six months after Julius and Ethel Rosenberg were arrested, the Justice Department was ready for trial. The indictment now read, "*United States of America v. Julius Rosenberg, Ethel Rosenberg, Anatoli A. Yakovlev, also known as "John," David Greenglass and Morton Sobell.*" Ruth Greenglass was named as an unindicted co-conspirator.

The government charged that Julius Rosenberg had recruited David Greenglass to spy at Los Alamos, that he had worked with Soviet vice consul Anatoli Yakovlev to send Harry Gold to Albuquerque to get the information from Greenglass, and that Ethel Rosenberg was a knowing witness and participant in these activities. The defense was unaware that if it made its case, the government planned to ask the judge to sentence to death the two individuals it saw as the leaders of the conspiracy, Julius and Ethel Rosenberg.

Irving R. Kaufman was the presiding judge for the Rosenberg trial. Kaufman had been a special assistant to the U.S. attorney general and was a great admirer of the FBI chief, J. Edgar Hoover.

Judge Kaufman was just forty years old when he presided over the Rosenberg case, which is very young for a judge to be assigned to such a high-profile case. But then Kaufman was an early achiever. He had been an exceptional student, earning his undergraduate degree from Fordham College at the age of eighteen. Although Jewish, he earned the nickname "Pope Kaufman" from his fellow students because of his excellence in the school's required Christian courses. Kaufman finished Fordham

Judge Irving R. Kaufman presided over the Rosenberg trial. He was only forty years old at the time of the trial, young for a judge assigned to such an important case.

Law School at age twenty, a year before he was old enough to take the bar exam.

As a Jew, Kaufman would later blunt criticism that anti-Semitism played a part in the Rosenbergs' trial. Indeed, a New York newspaper, the *Jewish Day*, argued in an editorial that the harsh sentence Kaufman imposed had been motivated by fears that he might be seen as being too lenient toward fellow Jews.

Irving Saypol, the lead attorney for the Justice Department, was the government's choice to lead the prosecution of the Rosenbergs and Sobell. From early in his career, Saypol was an eager prosecutor of Communists. He had already prosecuted other high-profile cases against suspected Communist spies. Saypol honestly believed that by pursuing Communists he was punishing evil—but he was not averse to basking in the favorable publicity generated by his work. Success in the Rosenberg trial would be likely to advance his career further.

The government's strategy was twofold. Saypol and his assistants would attempt to prove the charge of conspiracy. But to increase the likelihood of a conviction, they would also attempt to persuade the jury that the Rosenbergs and Sobell were guilty of a much more serious crime, treason (even though the indictment did not mention treason directly). Saypol announced in his opening argument that the defendants

> have committed the most serious crime which can be committed against the people of this country. [The defendants] conspired to deliver to the Soviet Union the weapons the Soviet Union could use to destroy us.[9]

To plant the idea of treason in the jurors' minds, Saypol would, throughout the trial, characterize the defendants as traitors:

> The defendants are party to an agreement to spy and steal from their own country [in the] interests of a foreign power which seeks to wipe it off the face of the earth. It would use the information from these traitors to destroy Americans and the people of the United States.[10]

The prosecution planned to use the anti-Communist hysteria afoot in the country to assist in making its case. At the time, many in the American public equated membership in the Communist Party with betrayal of the United States. Saypol hoped to use the connections the Rosenbergs and Sobell had with the Communist Party to persuade the jury that the defendants were likely to commit treason.

The Defense Prepares for Trial

From the outset, the Rosenbergs' attorney, Manny Bloch, underestimated the seriousness of the Rosenberg case. Bloch saw the conspiracy charges against the Rosenbergs as the government prosecutors' opening gambit, not as their bottom line. Bloch had defended clients in similar circumstances and had gotten them reduced charges and suspended sentences.

But Bloch was not entirely to blame for this miscalculation. The prosecution had not yet announced its intention to seek the death penalty, and he had not yet been confronted with Prosecutor Saypol's outright hostility to his clients. In addition, Bloch

Julius and Ethel Rosenberg leave the federal courthouse in New York after being indicted on charges of spying for the Soviet Union.

had no way of knowing how much the anti-Communist hysteria in the United States would dominate the trial and its aftermath, which would consume Bloch's time and attention not for the month or so he had guessed the trial would last, but for years.

A deputy marshal leads a handcuffed David Greenglass away from the courthouse. Greenglass testified that the Rosenbergs were leaders of the spy ring.

Manny Bloch's strategy included trying to discredit the testimony of the chief prosecution witnesses, Ruth and David Greenglass. On the surface, it seemed simple to show the jury that both David and Ruth were cooperating with the prosecutors in order to receive lenient sentences. Ruth was still recovering from the burns she had suffered in the fire, and had a new baby and a young child to care for. David was a devoted husband, and Bloch hoped to show how he would be desolated to be in prison where he would be unable to care for Ruth. In addition, Bloch planned to show the jury that Ruth and David Greenglass were seeking revenge in testifying against the Rosenbergs, because they both blamed Julius for the machine shop's failure.

Bloch also knew that he had to blunt what he expected would be the prosecution's main point of attack, the perception that because the Rosenbergs were Communists, they were probably guilty, no matter what the evidence might prove. Therefore Bloch's strategy would be to raise the issue of his clients' Communist Party membership at the outset, beating the prosecution to the punch.

The Greenglasses: Witnesses for the Prosecution

David and Ruth Greenglass, having already admitted their complicity in espionage, nevertheless hired John O. Rogge to represent

THE BATTLE BETWEEN SAYPOL AND KUNTZ

The enmity between Irving Saypol and Edward Kuntz began long before the two men faced one another during the Rosenberg trial. In 1936, Kuntz had been a member of a left-wing political party, the American Labor Party, while Saypol was just beginning his legal career. Even then, Saypol hated communism and did all he could to prevent Kuntz from running for a local political office.

When Kuntz lashed out at Saypol in his summation, claiming that Saypol had tried to "dig up poison" against his client, Morton Sobell, to make an innocent trip to Mexico appear to be a guilty flight, Saypol was enraged and planned to respond in kind during his own summation. He started to bring up Kuntz's membership in the American Labor Party. But Judge Kaufman interrupted, knowing that were Saypol to indicate his membership, it would have been the same as calling Kuntz a Communist, and Kaufman would have been forced to call a mistrial.

In a later interview, Roy Cohn, Saypol's assistant, claimed that he knew in advance of Saypol's plan to attack Kuntz and had warned the judge. If this version of events is true, this represented an improper ex parte communication. Such an exchange between the prosecution and a supposedly impartial judge might in itself have resulted in a mistrial, had the defense ever learned of it.

them. Rogge had once run for political office on a left-wing party's slate, and he was something of a celebrity in left-wing circles.

Because his clients had cooperated with the FBI and had pled guilty to the charges in the indictment, Rogge's role was straightforward. The government had promised a lenient sentence for David and a suspended sentence for Ruth. Rogge had to make sure that the government kept its word. And, more important, he must have felt he needed to protect the Greenglasses from attacks by the attorneys for the Rosenbergs, who he believed would lose no opportunity to avenge what they saw as his clients' betrayal of family members.

The Last Client: Morton Sobell

Morton Sobell had been imprisoned without bail since his forced return from Mexico. His wife, Helen, hired attorneys Edward Kuntz and Harold Phillips to defend him. Kuntz was well known for his defense of left-wing clients, and he was looking forward to a courtroom face-off with Saypol, who had once verbally attacked him at a meeting of the New York Bar Association.

Kuntz's central strategy was to attack the testimony of Elitcher and find any weaknesses he could in the prosecution's argument that Sobell's flight to Mexico was a sure sign of his guilt.

Chapter 3

The Trial Begins

NEW YORK CITY WAS DAMP and gloomy on Tuesday morning, March 6, 1951. For the entire opening day of the Rosenberg trial, the lights were on in the oak-paneled courtroom 7 of the federal courthouse on Manhattan's Foley Square. It was 9:30 when the panel of prospective jurors filed into the court.

All of Tuesday and Wednesday morning were devoted to impaneling a jury. As was the custom in federal trials, Judge Kaufman conducted jury questioning—called voir dire—himself. Jurors were dismissed from the panel if they were employees of, or knew anyone connected with, the FBI, or the House Un-American Activities Committee (HUAC), or if they had any connection with organizations either sympathetic to or opposed to communism. For example, one juror was dismissed because he had read a left-wing newspaper. Because the charges against the Rosenbergs carried the possibility of the death penalty, several other jurors were excused because they said that they opposed capital punishment. In addition, prospective jurors were dismissed if they had a relationship to any of the attorneys or defendants.

The eleven men and one woman who made up the jury had little in common besides their current task: deciding whether Sobell and the Rosenbergs were guilty or innocent. Among the jurors were five accountants, a retired civil servant, an electrician, two men in the food business, an estimator, and a sales manager. The lone woman was a housewife.

As the jury was being seated, Prosecutor Saypol, in one of his only personal, off-the-record remarks to the defense, told Manny

The jury in the Rosenberg trial stands outside the courthouse. These twelve citizens were responsible for deciding the Rosenbergs' guilt or innocence.

Bloch, "If your clients don't confess, they are doomed." [11] This open threat panicked Bloch, who, until that moment, had looked upon his job as trying to persuade the jury that communism did not equal disloyalty and trying to minimize the jail sentences his clients might get if convicted. Now Bloch knew that the Rosenbergs might face the death penalty.

In his opening statement, Saypol's reputation as an extreme anti-Communist did not desert him. He immediately made the defendants' Communist Party ties an issue, saying, "The evidence will show that the loyalty and the allegiance of the Rosenbergs and Sobell was not to our country but to Communism, Communism in this country and throughout the world." [12]

Emmanuel Bloch objected, arguing that communism was not on trial. But Kaufman overruled him, saying that bringing up the defendants' beliefs would be allowed as a means of showing their motivation for committing the acts they were accused of.

Saypol intensified his attack by invoking the specter of treason, telling the jury,

The evidence will show that these defendants joined with their co-conspirators in a deliberate, carefully planned conspiracy to deliver to the Soviet Union the information and the weapons the Soviet Union could use to destroy us. . . . The evidence of these treasonable acts of these three defendants you will find overwhelming. They have committed the most serious crime which can be committed against the people of this country.[13]

Manny Bloch's panic intensified: The prosecution had accused his clients of treason. Although a certain amount of overstatement is to be expected in an attorney's opening statements, alleging criminal acts that the defendants were not charged with, especially crimes that most certainly call for the death penalty, seemed to call for protest. Oddly, neither Bloch nor Sobell's attorneys objected to Saypol's tactics.

Testimony of Max Elitcher, Witness for the Prosecution

The prosecution called Max Elitcher as its first witness. He testified that, in 1944, when he was working for the Navy Ordnance

THE JURY AND THE SPECTER OF ANTI-SEMITISM

There were no Jewish jurors on the Rosenberg panel, a fact that, after the Rosenbergs' sentencing, caused much uproar within the Jewish community in the United States and elsewhere in the world when charges of anti-Semitism were first leveled at the prosecution. The *Indiana Jewish Chronicle* noted that "not a single jury member was Jewish, and this in the city of New York, which has a Jewish population amounting to one-third of the total population. Strange, or rather sinister, if you ask us."

Supporters of the Rosenbergs have argued that the absence of Jews on the panel was a result of deliberate prosecution strategy. In fact, both defense and prosecution lawyers excused potential jurors with obvious Jewish names. The defense worried about the potential of a Jewish juror proving what a good American he was by voting to convict; the prosecution worried about the more obvious sympathy vote. But the majority of panelists with Jewish surnames excused themselves because of their opposition to capital punishment.

Department, Sobell had invited him to join the Communist Party, and he had attended several party meetings. Elitcher said that Julius Rosenberg then approached him to ask him to help the Soviet Union.

Elitcher told the court that Rosenberg talked about the war and how the United States was harming the Soviet Union by denying it access to military items that might help the Soviets fight the Nazis. Rosenberg asked Elitcher if, in his job at the Bureau of Ordnance, he had access to anything that might help the Soviets.

Prosecutor Saypol then asked Elitcher to describe Morton Sobell's espionage activity. Elitcher testified that, in 1948, he went with Sobell to deliver some "valuable information" to Julius Rosenberg:

> Sobell said [the information] was too valuable to be destroyed and too dangerous to keep around. He said he wanted to deliver it to Rosenberg that night. He said he was tired and he wanted me to go along. He might not be able to make the trip back. He took a 35 millimeter film can. We drove to Catherine Slip [a waterfront street]. I parked the car facing the East River. He left with the can. I waited. He came back about a half hour later.[14]

Kuntz, Sobell's attorney, chose not to cross-examine Elitcher on his activities at Catherine Slip. Manny Bloch let Elitcher's testimony stand as well, questioning him only about his hopes of getting lenient treatment from the government in exchange for his testimony.

That afternoon, David Greenglass was scheduled to testify. It was his testimony that would form the heart of the prosecution's case.

The Testimony of David Greenglass: The Jell-O Box and the "Lens Mold"

Roy Cohn, Irving Saypol's assistant, led the interrogation of the state's next witness, David Greenglass. Cohn began by questioning Greenglass about the drawings he had made of the lens mold that he had given to Julius Rosenberg.

ROY COHN: CLIMBING TO THE TOP

Roy Cohn, a young assistant prosecutor in the Rosenberg trial, always sought the limelight. In addition to claiming that he had prevented Saypol from causing a mistrial, he told Radosh and Milton—authors of *The Rosenberg File*—that he was the one who went to Mexico to obtain information about Sobell's flight. And, after the jury returned its guilty verdict, he informed an FBI agent that Judge Kaufman "personally favored" the death penalty for Julius and Ethel Rosenberg.

Cohn would later gain fame as Senator Joseph McCarthy's right-hand man in the Army-McCarthy hearings, a fame that, when McCarthy fell from grace, also vanished.

U.S. senator Joseph McCarthy covers the microphones while speaking with chief counsel Roy Cohn. McCarthy was a leader of the hunt for Communists in America during the 1950s.

Greenglass began by testifying that Julius Rosenberg had informed him that a courier would meet Greenglass in Los Alamos to pick up any useful data he would be able to bring from his work at the Los Alamos A-bomb base. Here the jury learned about the cut-up Jell-O box used as a recognition signal and that it was Harry Gold who arrived in Albuquerque with the matching piece of the Jell-O box.

Greenglass told the court that he prepared some drawings of the lens mold for Gold, who took the material and left, paying Greenglass $500. Informing the court that his witness would be returning to testify further, Cohn excused Greenglass. Emmanuel Bloch, in cross-examining Greenglass, tried to make him look like someone incapable of making the drawings he had

David Greenglass prepares to testify for the prosecution. To avoid a long jail term, Greenglass told the court of the Rosenbergs' alleged role as leaders of an atomic spy ring.

supposedly made for Rosenberg. However, the strategy back-fired when Greenglass correctly answered technically worded questions in equally technical terms. Irving Saypol called his next witness, Walter Koski.

The Atomic Expert

Koski, a senior official of the U.S. Atomic Energy Commission (AEC), provided the prosecution's expert testimony. His job was to explain to the jury in nontechnical terms the function of the lens mold that Greenglass said he had sketched for Gold, thus proving the significance of the information the Rosenbergs had passed to the Soviets. The AEC and the prosecution had gone over Koski's testimony with a fine-tooth comb to avoid revealing any still-secret information.

Koski explained to the jury that, in order to detonate an atomic bomb, a smaller non-nuclear explosive device is needed. The lens mold sketched by Greenglass was used in the manu-facture of this device.

When Bloch cross-examined Koski, the expert revealed that the Greenglass sketches were not exact enough to serve as blue-prints. But Koski maintained that the drawings nevertheless provided more information than the AEC would have wanted an enemy to have about what was being built at Los Alamos.

Greenglass Back on the Stand

On Monday morning, Greenglass took the stand again, testifying that, when he returned to New York in the fall of 1945, he and his wife, Ruth, drove to Rosenberg's home and gave him a cross-sectional drawing of the bomb the United States dropped on Nagasaki on August 7, 1945. At the prosecution's request, Greenglass had prepared copies of his original drawings, with what he characterized as a reasonably accurate description of the bomb. What followed turned out to be a gift to the prosecution.

When Roy Cohn attempted to introduce the drawings as evi-dence, Bloch objected on the grounds that the material—which he had not seen, nor could he understand—was of too sensitive a nature to be revealed to the court. This was a major error on

Shown is a "Fat Man" nuclear bomb similar to those used on Japan near the end of World War II. This was one of the many top secret projects housed at the Los Alamos facilities.

the part of the defense. By objecting to the prosecution's attempt to make such highly sensitive material public, Bloch had confirmed for the jury the critical importance of the drawings.

Although astonished by Bloch's error, Saypol was also pleased. He made a dig at Bloch, saying that it was "a very strange request coming from the defendants."

Bloch replied, "Not a strange request coming from me at the present." [15]

Sobell's lawyers, Kuntz and Phillips, were outraged. This characterization of the drawings could only hurt their client. Phillips objected to impounding the evidence, saying, "I do not feel that an attorney for a defendant in a criminal case should make concessions which will save the prosecution from the necessity of proving things which we may be able to refute." [16] Kaufman overruled the objection. With the jury no doubt impressed at how the defense, as well as the prosecution, perceived David Greenglass's crude drawings as important atomic secrets, Julius and Ethel Rosenberg began to look like enemies of the United States.

The Testimony of Ruth Greenglass: The Woman Scorning

The prosecution was sure that David Greenglass's wife, Ruth, would be a sympathetic witness. It intended to portray Ruth Greenglass as a young mother concerned for her family and fearful that her brother-in-law was leading them into disaster with his espionage activities.

James Kilsheimer, another of Irving Saypol's assistants, led the examination of Ruth Greenglass. He drew from her the most significant testimony regarding the depth of Ethel Rosenberg's involvement in her husband's espionage. Kilsheimer asked Ruth about one of her and David's visits to his sister and brother-in-law in New York while he was on furlough from the army:

> KILSHEIMER: What did you say to Ethel Rosenberg at that time?
>
> GREENGLASS: Well, Ethel said that she was tired, and I asked her what she had been doing. She said she had been typing; and I asked her if she had found David's notes hard to distinguish. She said no, she was used to his handwriting. Then she said that Julie [Julius], too, was tired; that he was very busy; he ran around a good deal; that all his time and his energies were used in this thing [his espionage activities]; that was the most important thing to him.[17]

Ruth Greenglass went on to testify about the day Harry Gold showed up at their apartment in Albuquerque bearing the cut-up Jell-O box. Prosecutor Kilsheimer asked, "Where was the last time you had seen the portion of the Jell-O box side which Harry Gold produced?"

Ruth Greenglass replied, "In Julius Rosenberg's hand."[18]

Then Ruth Greenglass testified that, while staying in the Rosenbergs' apartment, she noticed a mahogany console table that Ethel told her was a "gift from a friend,"[19] a phrase Ruth said she understood to mean Julius Rosenberg's Soviet handler, or agent in New York directly overseeing spy activities and reporting results to Moscow. Greenglass testified that Julius turned the console over to show a hollowed section underneath with a place for a lamp. She said that Julius told her the console was used to microfilm Ethel's typewritten notes, although exactly how this piece of furniture was actually used was never made clear in the trial.

Ruth Greenglass also testified that just before the FBI had brought them in for questioning, Julius had given them $4,000 and warned her and her husband to flee the country. Ruth told the court that they instead gave the money to their attorney as a retainer.

Alexander Bloch, Manny Bloch's father, who was serving as Ethel Rosenberg's lawyer, cross-examined Ruth Greenglass. His aim was to undermine her testimony by having her go over it again, hoping that her repetition of exact phrases would indicate to the jury how the FBI and the prosecution had coached her.

Ruth Greenglass testified that Julius and Ethel Rosenberg were key links in the Soviet spy ring.

THE CONSOLE TABLE:
FROM MACY'S OR MOSCOW?

The console table is one of the more controversial elements of the Rosenberg trial. Ruth Greenglass claimed it was an espionage device provided by the Soviets, whereas Rosenberg later testified that it was just an ordinary table that his wife had purchased at Macy's department store.

The table itself was not introduced into evidence, because—despite a thorough FBI search—it could not be found in time to be used as evidence in the trial. Even though it is unclear how its "hollowed-out section" could aid in the photographing of documents, if the prosecution could have produced the table as Ruth described it, the table's existence alone would have been concrete evidence of the Rosenbergs' guilt.

Then, in 1953, as Julius and Ethel waited on death row, the table turned up. It had been in the basement of Julius's mother, Sophie Rosenberg. Mrs. Cox, the maid who had testified about the table, said she recognized it, but she refused to sign an affidavit saying so. Macy's employees attested to the fact that it had been bought at their store. But the table did not turn out to be a smoking gun. It had no "hollowed-out" place in it.

And yet the mystery surrounding this table remains. The FBI occasionally made audio recordings of visits between the Rosenbergs and their friends and supporters. On one such visit, Julius's sister asked Ethel about the table. Ethel Rosenberg grew angry, ordering her sister-in-law, "Don't mention that table in here! It doesn't concern you!"

A. BLOCH: Are you aware of the fact that the narrative you just gave us is almost identical with the verbiage used on your first giving of the testimony of that particular occurrence?

GREENGLASS: No, I am not.[20]

But neither Saypol nor Judge Kaufman would allow Bloch's strategy to go unchallenged.

SAYPOL: Just a moment. I appreciate so expert an opinion as to the accuracy of the witness's recollection, but I object to the form of the question.

COURT: Your objection is sustained. I don't know exactly what the point is. If the witness had left out something,

Mr. Bloch would say that the witness had left out something. Mr. Bloch would say that the witness didn't repeat the story accurately. And the witness repeats it accurately, and apparently that isn't any good.[21]

Finally, Manny Bloch cross-examined Ruth Greenglass about the $4,000 that Julius had given the Greenglasses. Bloch attempted to get Ruth to say that the money was in repayment of a business debt. But Ruth stuck to her story, insisting that Julius had told them the money was to finance their flight from the United States.

The Testimony of Harry Gold

The prosecution's next witness was Harry Gold, a self-confessed spy. Saypol needed to establish a link between the Soviets, the Greenglasses, and the Rosenbergs—and Gold was that link. Harry Gold was the courier between Julius Rosenberg and Soviet agent Anatoli Yakovlev, the KGB's chief of U.S. spy operations. Yakovlev had been named in the indictment along with the Rosenbergs and Sobell.

Short, stoop-shouldered, with deep-set eyes, Harry Gold was not physically imposing. However, his educated speech and obvious intelligence made him seem a credible witness. But in fact, Harry Gold was a somewhat unreliable witness. At various times, he had concocted stories about his imaginary family and about his success as a master spy and other exploits that later proved to be entirely fictional. At the time he testified against the Rosenbergs, in fact, he was under indictment for perjury in an earlier espionage case in which he had served as a witness.

Gold had already been tried, convicted, and sentenced for his crimes so, unlike the other prosecution witnesses, he had nothing to gain from testifying, a fact that the prosecution lost no time in establishing. Even though Gold was the Greenglasses' contact, Gold insisted that he had never met the Rosenbergs, despite the fact that he had told the FBI about an abortive meeting in February 1950 in which, arriving at the appointed place, he had seen a man who looked like Julius Rosenberg on the

Harry Gold is shown being escorted by two federal officers. Prosecutors used his testimony to establish a link between the Rosenbergs and Anatoli Yakovlev, the Soviet Union's chief of spy operations in the United States.

other side of the street. The prosecution did not raise this attempted meeting at the trial, perhaps because Gold's description of the man was inconclusive. Gold was, however, able to describe in detail a particular meeting he had with his Soviet handler Yakovlev in a seedy bar in Manhattan. There Yakovlev gave Gold his instructions for the trip to Albuquerque, New Mexico, to get information from David Greenglass.

> HARRY GOLD: Yakovlev then gave me a piece of paper [with] the name "Greenglass." Then a number [on] "High Street.". . . The last thing that was on the paper was: "Recognition signal: I come from Julius." [22]

This testimony was devastating for the defense. Harry Gold, an admitted spy, had used the name "Julius" as a code word.

Gold further testified about his meeting with both Ruth and David Greenglass at their apartment

> and his receipt of "three or four handwritten pages plus a couple of sketches. The sketches had letters on them which were referred to in the text of the three or four handwritten pages. The sketches appeared to be for a device of some kind." [23]

Gold's testimony had now connected the Rosenbergs and the Greenglasses to a real spy ring, guided by none other than Anatoli Yakovlev, the chief Soviet spy in the United States.

In his cross-examination, Bloch failed to challenge Gold's testimony, except to point out that Gold, one of the top conspirators, had never met Rosenberg, had never seen him, had never had any contact with him. But Gold's use of the phrase "I come from Julius" hovered in the courtroom.

The Testimony of Elizabeth Bentley

The prosecution's final witness was Elizabeth Bentley, a one time Soviet agent and the lover of Jacob Golos, the man who preceded Yakovlev as the chief Russian spy in the United States. Bentley, called the "Red Spy Queen" by the press, was something of a celebrity. She had become an informer for the U.S. government and had begun writing articles and books about her undercover exploits.

Bentley's contribution to the prosecution's case was minimal. In 1942, she testified, she had gone with Golos to meet with someone near the Knickerbocker Village neighborhood. She said that she had waited in the car while the meeting took place and was too far away to see the man but recalled that Golos had identified him as Julius.

Under questioning from Assistant Prosecutor Myles Lane and Kilsheimer, Bentley then testified that in 1943 and 1944 she had spoken several times over the telephone to a man who identified himself as "Julius" and who asked to get in touch with Jacob Golos.

Why Saypol included Bentley in his list of witnesses is unclear. In putting together the case against the Rosenbergs, neither the FBI nor Saypol's assistant Roy Cohn saw any benefit in having Bentley testify, but Saypol had persisted. One theory is that Saypol hoped to benefit personally from the publicity that Bentley would draw. Observers have suggested that Bentley's appearance, attended as it was by reporters and photographers, would allow the prosecution—and in particular, Chief Prosecutor Saypol to be seen in a flattering light. Whatever the prosecution's motives for having her testify, Bentley's mention of a mysterious man named "Julius," now important enough to

Former Soviet agent Elizabeth Bentley testified that in 1943 and 1944 she had spoken to a man calling himself "Julius" who wished to make contact with a known Soviet spy, Jacob Golos.

be a contact for top Soviet spy Jacob Golos as well as his successor, Yakovlev, put Julius Rosenberg at the center of a spy ring whose reach extended into the most closely guarded of U.S. secrets, the development of the atomic bomb.

On cross-examination, Bloch managed to raise some doubts about Bentley's story by forcing her to admit that the quest for publicity, not the quest for justice, was her motive in testifying. As he questioned her, Bloch argued that Bentley had invented her connection to the Rosenbergs and was testifying so that she could sell more books.

While Bentley did admit that she mentioned the "Julius" incident in her yet-to-be-published book, she could not recall if she had written that particular part before or after questioning by the FBI. On that inconclusive note, Elizabeth Bentley left the stand.

In their book *The Rosenberg File*, Radosh and Milton suggest that Bloch might have gained an advantage by subpoenaing Bentley's manuscript and discovering that the incident was *not* in the book. He could then have argued that the stories of Golos's meeting and the phone calls had been cooked up between Bentley, who could sell more books by her connection with a newsworthy trial, and the FBI, who could put another nail in its case against Rosenberg. But, for reasons that are unclear, Bloch did not follow up on this possible line of questioning.

ELIZABETH BENTLEY

In their book *The Rosenberg File: A Search for the Truth*, Radosh and Milton reveal that, in a document released in 1975 under the Freedom of Information Act, Elizabeth Bentley had been talking to the FBI about the mysterious "Julius" as early as 1945. In her discussions with interrogators, Bentley revealed:

> I was driving with GOLOS when he stopped the car to meet someone. I managed to get a fleeting glance at this individual and I recall that he was tall, thin, and wore horn rimmed eyeglasses [like Julius Rosenberg]. GOLOS told me he gave this person my residence telephone number so that he would be able to reach GOLOS whenever he desired. He [GOLOS] did not elaborate on the activities of this person nor did he identify any of them, except that this one man to whom he gave my telephone number was referred to as "JULIUS."

The Prosecution Rests

The prosecution called a few final witnesses before completing its case. The first was the Rosenbergs' family doctor, George Bernhardt, who testified that Rosenberg called him in May 1950 to inquire about the kinds of inoculations required for a trip to Mexico. Saypol would later argue in his summation that Rosenberg was asking about the shots in order to help Morton Sobell and his family prepare for their flight.

The next witness was William Danziger, who admitted forwarding Sobell's mail to Mexico using the aliases "Morton Sowell" and "Morton Levitov."

The prosecution wrapped up its case with some minor witnesses. Minerva Espinoza, an optical store clerk from Vera Cruz, Mexico, testified that Sobell used the alias "Morris Sand" when he came into her shop for a pair of glasses. Hotel clerks José Broccado Vendrell and Dora Bautista said that Sobell had used other aliases when he checked into hotels in the Mexican cities of Vera Cruz and Tampico. And James Huggins, an immigration service guard, said that he had witnessed Sobell's "deportation" from Mexico. Colonel Lansdale, head of Los Alamos Security, told the jury about security precautions at the base, and John Derry, from the AEC, testified about technical details of the lens mold sketches.

Before noon on March 20, 1951, the prosecution rested its case, retaining the right to call rebuttal witnesses after the defense had presented its case.

Chapter 4

The Defense's Turn

FROM THE OUTSET, THE Rosenbergs' defense team lacked the resources to mount an adequate effort on their behalf. Nobody on the defense team was an expert on atomic energy, for example. Gloria Agrin, Manny Bloch's assistant, told journalist Ted Morgan in 1975 that both she and Bloch thought the lens mold had something to do with photography. "We learned about implosion at the same time as the jury. We had no background in physics or science." [24] Had he known how vague they actually were, Bloch would not have needed to call for the impoundment of the sketches. He also might have been able to guess how much the prosecution was worried about having to defend Greenglass's crude drawings, made from memory six years after the fact.

Despite their handicaps, it was the defense team's turn to make the case for their clients' innocence, a job made much harder by the national mood of anti-Communist hysteria. Although the American system of justice is based on the principle that a defendant is innocent until proven guilty, creating reasonable doubt about the defendants' guilt would not be enough to achieve an acquittal in this case.

In addition to their other difficulties, the defense had one insurmountable problem: the clients themselves. In retrospect, even people who believed in the Rosenbergs' innocence admit that the couple might have seemed less than sympathetic to the jurors. First, they were alleged Communists, and in America in 1951, an accused Communist was thought to be capable of almost any heinous act. The constitutional guarantee that Americans are free to associate with whoever they please did not seem to apply to Communists. In

THE LENS MOLD: VITAL SECRET
OR VAGUE SKETCH?

Many observers, in years since the trial, have pointed out the absurdity of the government's argument that David Greenglass, a machinist with a high school education, would have the technical knowledge to make useful drawings of such a sophisticated device as the lens mold. The government's release of Greenglass's drawing only serves to strengthen that view.

Much of Greenglass's information about the workings of the device, and the atomic bomb (gleaned from pretrial rehearsals by government and AEC coaches), was in fact wrong. Emmanuel Bloch missed his chance to attack the prosecution's case by forcing the government to prove the importance of Greenglass's drawings. He later claimed that he lacked the expertise to challenge this testimony.

In 1954, General Leslie Groves, the man who was so wrong in his predictions of when the Russians would have their own nuclear device, told a closed meeting of the AEC, "The data that went out in the case of the Rosenbergs was of minor value."

a newspaper survey of the time, more than 50 percent of those interviewed agreed that "all known Communists should be jailed." [25]

To make matters worse, Julius and Ethel Rosenberg were not the most appealing of witnesses. From the beginning, commentators had pointed out how cold and remote both defendants appeared. To observers, it seemed that the Rosenbergs thought themselves superior to the entire proceeding. Their attitude kept them from seeing how they might appear to a jury caught up in the anti-Communist hysteria of the times. Even had the jury wanted to sympathize with the defendants, they would have found it difficult under the arrogant stare of Julius and the haughty demeanor of Ethel Rosenberg.

The defense team had discussed how to handle an issue that they were sure would come up: what to do when the prosecution asked the Rosenbergs about their membership in the Communist Party. Manny Bloch, calling on his years of experience defending Communist and other politically unpopular clients, argued that the Rosenbergs should invoke their Fifth Amendment right against self-incrimination to avoid turning the trial into one in which the Communist Party was at issue.

Outside the White House, hundreds of men and women demonstrate in favor of the death penalty for the Rosenbergs.

Alexander Bloch disagreed. He had no background in political trials, but he knew how to read a jury. This one, he was sure, believed as did many Americans, that if a defendant "took the fifth," then he must be guilty.

But both Manny Bloch and the Rosenbergs insisted that they invoke their Fifth Amendment rights. Julius in particular was concerned that given an opening, the prosecution would ask about their friends in the Communist groups to which they belonged. In his book *The Judgment of Julius and Ethel Rosenberg,* John Wexley noted that neither Rosenberg was willing to face a barrage of hostile questions about their friends in the Communist Party. Despite these pitfalls, there seemed no alternative to allowing the Rosenbergs to testify in their own defense.

Julius Rosenberg for the Defense

By the time he was called to testify in his own defense, Julius Rosenberg had spent eight months in prison and had endured tremendous pressure from the government to confess to spying for the Soviets. The Justice Department had guaranteed Rosenberg that both he and his wife would receive the death penalty if he refused to cooperate.

But this pressure had only made Rosenberg more sure of the rightness of his cause and had convinced him that he was an innocent victim of a system of justice corrupted by political hysteria. Julius Rosenberg believed not only that he was innocent but that history would agree with him.

THE FIFTH AMENDMENT: PROTECTING THE INNOCENT OR SHIELDING THE GUILTY?

When Julius and Ethel Rosenberg asserted their rights against self-incrimination, they were claiming the protection of the Fifth Amendment to the U.S. Constitution.

No amendment to the Constitution has engendered as much controversy as the Fifth Amendment. It deals with the rights of accused criminals by providing for due process of law, forbidding double jeopardy (trying someone twice for the same offense), and stating that no person may be forced to testify as a witness against himself or herself.

The Fifth Amendment earned its controversial reputation during the 1950s and '60s, when it was invoked by individuals accused of subversive activities and membership in organized crime. Because of the temper of the times, and the frustration with a legal system that seemed to offer more protection for criminals than for victims, the public and the press began to see "taking the fifth" as virtually equivalent to an admission of guilt.

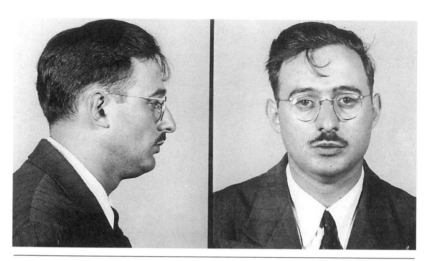

These photos show Julius Rosenberg shortly before the beginning of the espionage trial.

On Wednesday, March 21, Julius Rosenberg began his testimony in his own defense. Manny Bloch began his direct examination of his client by asking him to contradict David and Ruth Greenglass's testimony:

E. BLOCH: Did you ever have any conversation with Mrs. Ruth Greenglass at or about that time with respect to getting information from Dave Greenglass out of the place that he was working?

ROSENBERG: I did not.

E. BLOCH: Did you know in the middle of November 1944 where Dave Greenglass was stationed?

ROSENBERG: I did not.

E. BLOCH: Did you know in the middle of November 1944 that there was such a project known as the Los Alamos Project?

ROSENBERG: I did not.

E. BLOCH: Did you ever give Ruth Greenglass $250, for her to go out to visit her husband in New Mexico, for the purpose of trying to enlist him in espionage work?

ROSENBERG: I did not.[26]

Bloch then led Rosenberg through each incident claimed in the indictment, and Rosenberg denied each of them. The attorney was trying to turn the Greenglasses' damaging testimony into a credibility contest, making the jury decide Rosenberg's guilt based on whether they believed him or his in-laws.

This might have been a good strategy had the jury been inclined to sympathize with Rosenberg. But Judge Kaufman intervened, interrupting Bloch's direct examination with questions of his own:

COURT: Well, did you ever belong to any group that discussed the system of Russia?

ROSENBERG: Well, your Honor, I feel at this time that I refuse to answer a question that might tend to incriminate me.[27]

MANNY BLOCH'S FATEFUL ERROR

Most observers agree that Emmanuel Bloch severely damaged his defense by asking that the drawings be kept secret from the jury and the press. The drawings were, after all, only copies created by Greenglass from memory—at the request of the prosecution—six years later. Most experts have claimed that Greenglass's drawings—whether they were originals or copies—would be useless for anyone who wanted to actually make an atomic bomb.

Bloch then proceeded to make matters worse. He agreed to stipulate that the drawings and other material Greenglass claimed to have given the Rosenbergs were indeed secret and related to the national defense, thus saving the prosecution the trouble of proving it. Although Bloch claimed that he was acting as a patriotic American—hoping that his clients would be seen that way as well—to the jury his action only made Greenglass seem like a more reliable witness and the crime the Rosenbergs were accused of that much more serious.

In their book *The Rosenberg File*, Radosh and Milton speculate that Bloch's act was that of a desperate man. He saw his case as already lost and so was trying for jury sympathy, at least as far as averting the death penalty.

Without the prosecution even having to cross-examine him, Rosenberg was demonstrating to the jury that he had something to hide.

Unable to force Rosenberg to admit to being a Communist, Kaufman questioned Julius Rosenberg about his political ideas:

> KAUFMAN: Did you ever discuss . . . the respective preferences of the economic systems between the United States and Russia?[28]

Rosenberg replied that he had discussed such matters in normal conversation, and he believed that both systems had positive aspects.

Bloch then questioned Rosenberg about his version of events surrounding the machine shop he had owned with David Greenglass, in the process making the point that David Greenglass kept asking for money because his wife was nagging him about it. By portraying Greenglass as a stereotypical henpecked husband, Bloch was trying to help the jury see David Greenglass as a weak-willed, easily manipulated man whose wife was a greedy spendthrift. Ruth Greenglass's greed, Bloch argued, was the cause of the rift that led the Greenglasses to testify against their in-laws.

Then it was the prosecution's turn to question Rosenberg. Saypol made the most of his opening, asking Rosenberg about his Communist affiliations, starting with his student days at City College of New York. Saypol's apparent goal was to force Rosenberg to repeatedly take the fifth, reminding the jurors—in case they had forgotten—the kind of man to whom they were listening.

Then, near the end of his cross-examination, Saypol asked Rosenberg, almost casually, did you "in the month of June 1950, or May 1950, have any passport photos taken of yourself?" [29]

Rosenberg replied that he had not. Saypol pressed on, mentioning the address of the photographer, at 99 Park Row. Then, faced with this specific information, Rosenberg changed his mind, saying that he might have visited there, having been in many photographers' shops.

Julius Rosenberg arrives at the federal courthouse for yet another day of the trial.

Saypol continued his line of questioning, asking Rosenberg if he had been alone or with his family, and what he had told the photographer on the occasion of his visit. When Rosenberg again failed to recall saying anything, Saypol suggested that Rosenberg had said he was getting passport photos for a trip to France to collect an inheritance. Again Rosenberg denied that he had said any such thing. But Saypol had led Rosenberg from his initial denial that he had ever had pictures taken to a discussion of what he had told a certain photographer in a shop on Park Row in May or June of 1950—a few days after he had been questioned by the FBI. Any credibility the defendant might have possessed was destroyed.

Last Chance for Life: Ethel Rosenberg

Once Julius Rosenberg had finished testifying, it was Ethel Rosenberg's turn. Her attorney, Alexander Bloch, might have thought he had an easier task of defending Ethel Rosenberg than his son had had in defending her husband. He had to make the jury empathize with Ethel as a normal young wife and mother and to allow her to rebut the testimony of her brother and sister-in-law.

Alexander Bloch set out to accomplish the first part of his strategy by asking Ethel Rosenberg about raising children and running a household, implying that she was much too busy with domestic duties to take part in the activities of a spy ring. In addition, he reached for the jury's sympathy by asking her about her children. Ethel answered that they were at a temporary shelter and that she had not seen them since she was arrested.

Alexander Bloch's other strategy was to have Ethel Rosenberg rebut the Greenglasses' testimony. Ruth Greenglass had accused her sister-in-law of typing up David Greenglass's notes on the atomic bomb using an old typewriter. To try and turn this typewriter into an innocent family possession, Alexander Bloch asked Ethel if she had purchased it when she was a teenager. Again, Judge Kaufman interrupted, asking if Ethel had ever used the typewriter to write a letter concerning her husband's firing from the Signal Corps.

KAUFMAN: What was the situation about?

ETHEL ROSENBERG: Well, it was alleged that he was a member of the Communist Party.

KAUFMAN: And he was dismissed for that reason?

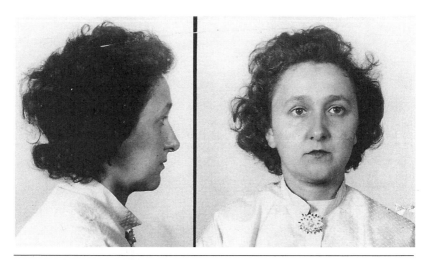

Ethel Rosenberg, when called upon to testify, asserted her Fifth Amendment protection against self-incrimination.

ETHEL ROSENBERG: I refuse to answer on the ground that this might be incriminating.[30]

As it had with Julius, Judge Kaufman's questioning made Ethel Rosenberg look as though she had something to hide.

In another tactic to gain sympathy for his client, Alexander Bloch asked a series of questions designed to show that both Ethel and her son Robert were too ill during the period of alleged espionage work for Ethel to have played a very active role.

ETHEL ROSENBERG: Well, it so happens that I have had a spinal curvature since I was about thirteen and every once in a while that has given me some trouble, and at that time it began to kick up again, and occasionally I have to get into bed and nurse a severe backache. It finally got so bad that I went to visit my doctor.

A. BLOCH: And what was the condition of your child's health?

ETHEL ROSENBERG: The condition of my child was very poor. I had had a very difficult time ever since his birth, I mean, with him. He was given to severe cold and sore throat with high fever. It wasn't the usual thing of where a baby gets sick occasionally. It was practically every week in and week out.[31]

In an additional attempt to counteract the Greenglasses' damaging testimony, Alexander Bloch read aloud from the trial transcript Ruth's statements about such things as the Jell-O box recognition signal and the $4,000. Ethel denied any knowledge of these events.

A. BLOCH: Did you ever hear of any such thing as a Jell-O box being cut in two in order to be a means of identification of any emissary or agent to be sent by your husband out West in order to get information from the Los Alamos Project?

ETHEL ROSENBERG: Outside of this courtroom, I never heard of any such thing.[32]

But despite his best efforts, it was difficult for Bloch to arouse sympathy for Ethel among the jurors. In addition to Kaufman's efforts to remind the jurors that she was a Communist, Ethel's demeanor on the witness stand was unlikely to gain her much sympathy. As Radosh and Milton point out,

Beneath [Ethel's] composure was a barely concealed contempt for the whole proceedings, which no doubt counted heavily against her when the jury came to weigh her testimony. The same sexist stereotypes that might have disposed the jury to feel sorry for a wronged woman dragged into a serious crime out of loyalty to her husband could easily be turned against a woman who failed to display the proper signs of victimization.[33]

Unfortunately for Julius Rosenberg, the more Alexander Bloch painted Ethel as a victim, the more it made her husband appear to have taken advantage of his wife's loyalty. And Ethel was loyal to her husband, to the very end.

In his cross-examination, Saypol began right away to ruffle Ethel's composure, making her seem nervous, ill at ease, and

Julius Rosenberg, escorted by a deputy marshal, appears, with Ethel at his side, for the trial's opening in March 1951.

hostile. He began by asking her the same questions he had asked Julius about the photographs they had had taken in May or June of 1950. Ethel Rosenberg, like her husband, was vague about the shop where they had their pictures taken, but she was sure that they had not been passport photos.

Following a line of questioning about Ethel's frequent efforts to help her brother, David Greenglass, with his financial problems, Saypol seized the opportunity to accuse Ethel Rosenberg of being a Communist.

SAYPOL: You said you did everything to help [your brother], do you remember that?

ETHEL ROSENBERG: Yes.

SAYPOL: Did you help him join the Communist Party? . . .

ETHEL ROSENBERG: I am going to refuse to answer on the ground of self-incrimination.[34]

Saypol's strategy of forcing the defendants to seek shelter behind the Fifth Amendment was working. It would be very difficult for a juror not to conclude that Ethel Rosenberg was hiding something.

On redirect, in which an attorney gets a second chance to question his or her witness, Manny Bloch (taking over from his father) tried desperately to minimize the damage to Ethel by getting her to repeat that she considered herself innocent of the charges against her. Judge Kaufman, however, did not let the matter rest.

GRAND JURIES: THE AMERICAN INQUISITION

A grand jury is a group of people who are selected and sworn in by a court, just like jurors who are chosen to serve on a trial. But grand juries differ from trial juries in several ways.

For one thing, grand juries may hear several cases. In the federal system, a grand jury can hear cases over a term of up to thirty-six months. Unlike trial juries, grand juries do not decide if someone is guilty of criminal charges that have been brought against him or her. Grand juries listen to evidence and decide if someone should be charged with a crime. The grand jury that heard witnesses and prosecutors in the Rosenberg case decided that there was enough evidence against the conspirators to warrant a trial, so they returned indictments against the defendants, which allowed the government to proceed with the prosecution.

ETHEL ROSENBERG: I didn't believe I was guilty then [at the time of her grand jury testimony], I don't believe it today. As a matter of fact, I know I wasn't guilty then, and I know I am not guilty now.

KAUFMAN: The point is, you answered these questions at the trial and you refused to [earlier] on the grounds that it would tend to incriminate you before the grand jury.

ETHEL ROSENBERG: As I said before, I can't remember now what reasons I might or might not have had to use the grounds of self-incrimination then.[35]

Despite the firmness of her responses to Kaufman's questions, Ethel Rosenberg's credibility was shaken.

The Silence of Morton Sobell

Aside from Anatoli Yakovlev, who had evaded capture and was back in the Soviet Union, the last defendant named in the government's indictment was Morton Sobell, the fugitive who had been forcibly returned from Mexico.

Sobell's attorney Edward Kuntz had a great deal of experience defending left-wing and Communist clients. But he, like Bloch, faced several problems defending this particular client. For one thing, Sobell was not even mentioned in the twelve overt acts cited in the indictment, and, despite his efforts, Kuntz could not get the government to reveal any of the particulars of the accusations against his client. Prosecutors would reveal only that Sobell was charged with having conversations with Julius Rosenberg growing out of a conspiracy in which he (Sobell) had participated. The vagueness of the charges gave Kuntz very little to work with.

Second, Sobell's relationship with his attorneys was chilly. This, Sobell later admitted, hurt his chance in court. Sobell suggests in his book, *On Doing Time*, that their relationship was strained because neither Kuntz nor Harold Phillips, his associate, was convinced of his innocence.

Finally, there was the issue of Sobell's flight to Mexico. Even though the defense team suspected that the FBI was

Deputy Marshal Eugene Fitzgerald brings Morton Sobell (left) to court.

involved in Sobell's being kidnapped in Mexico and forced to return to the United States, which violated a number of international treaties, making that charge was not likely to earn points with the jury. That strategy could even backfire by suggesting to the jury just how important the FBI considered Sobell to be. Kuntz therefore decided not to have Sobell testify at all, and on this note, the defense rested. The trial, however, was not over.

The Prosecution's Surprise: The Testimony of Ben Schneider

In a criminal trial, the prosecution gets the final word, called rebuttal. For this phase of the trial, Saypol called a surprise witness, Ben Schneider, who stunned the defense by testifying that he was the photographer in the shop on Park Row who took passport-type photographs of Julius and Ethel Rosenberg and their children. Schneider further claimed that Rosenberg had told him that he and his family were "going to France; there was some property left; they were going to take care of it—that is, his wife was left some property." [36] Schneider also swore that he had not seen either of the Rosenbergs since that day, until his appearance on the witness stand.

Manny Bloch objected to Schneider's entire testimony and moved for a mistrial. Schneider had not been on the government's list of prospective witnesses; the defense, he protested, had had no chance to prepare a cross-examination. The prosecution replied that the shop owner had been found only the day before and admitted that he had no records, such as receipts or negatives, to back up his story. However, Sobell's flight to Mexico and news of other suspected spies' disappearance, coupled with Schneider's testimony, left the impression with the jury

SCHNEIDER: WHERE DID HE COME FROM?

The FBI found Ben Schneider, the photographer who later testified that he had taken passport photos of the Rosenbergs, with the aid of a fellow prisoner of Julius Rosenberg who was an FBI informant.

The truth of how Schneider was discovered was revealed in FBI files made available in 1975 under the Freedom of Information Act. Eugene Jerome Tartakow was a prisoner in the Tombs serving a two-year sentence for auto theft at the same time that Julius Rosenberg was imprisoned there awaiting trial. The two became friends and confidants while playing chess together.

One thing that Tartakow did *not* confide in Rosenberg was that he had approached the FBI and offered to tell them what Rosenberg told *him*. Tartakow sent a note to the FBI saying that Julius was worried that the FBI might locate the photographer who took passport photos of him and his family.

Tartakow would later claim that he was trying to "rescue" Rosenberg from his own unbending stance by giving the FBI information that might save his life. But the FBI reports reveal that he was also seeking to receive an early release from jail in exchange for being an informant.

that the Rosenbergs had intended to leave the country. Judge Kaufman ignored defense protests and Bloch's motion for a mistrial, and the trial went on. Kaufman ordered both prosecution and defense to return on the following day, Wednesday, March 28, 1951, for jury instructions and final summations.

Chapter 5

The Battle for Life

THE FINAL WORDS FROM THE prosecution and defense—the summations—represent the last chance for either the prosecution or defense to make any points not made during the trial itself and to reinforce earlier arguments. The trial's outcome is unlikely to be changed by a summation, however. Often, most members of the jury have already made up their minds. By the time of summations in *United States of America v. Julius Rosenberg, Ethel Rosenberg, Anatoli Yakovlev, also known as "John," David Greenglass and Morton Sobell*, the defense had already lost. And they knew it.

The defense had lost even though David and Ruth Greenglass and Harry Gold, the witnesses who testified for the prosecution, were themselves either accused or confessed spies. The defense had lost even though the prosecution could produce no physical evidence of espionage or conspiracy—no documents, film, or drawings. And the defense had lost even though Julius and Ethel Rosenberg had taken the witness stand and denied resolutely that they were spies.

The Last Stand of the Defense

When Manny Bloch addressed the jury and the spectators packed into the courtroom on Wednesday, March 28, 1951, he did so with the air of a man who knew he was doomed, but who was still going to do his best.

Bloch knew he had made several errors: moving to keep the Greenglass documents secret, failing to challenge Harry Gold's testimony, and, perhaps most significant, failing to realize how large a role the nation's anti-Communist paranoia would play in the trial.

Bloch also knew he had almost no chance to correct these errors. So Bloch appealed to the jurors' emotions. He began with what must have seemed an insincere expression of gratitude to Judge Kaufman: "I would like to say to the Court that we feel you have treated us with the utmost courtesy." To the prosecution, he stated, "I would also like to say to the members of Mr. Saypol's staff that we are appreciative of the courtesies extended to us." [37]

In his summation, Bloch got right to what he believed was the real issue of the trial, the issue that, although unspoken, hung over everything that had happened inside the courtroom: communism. Ignoring the stories of trips to New Mexico, of money changing hands, of console tables or drawings and documents, Bloch appealed to the jury:

> Please don't decide this case because you may have some bias or some prejudice. . . . [If] you want to convict these defendants because you think they are Communists, and you don't like communism and you don't like any member of the Communist Party, then, ladies and gentlemen, I can sit down now and there is absolutely no use in my talking. [38]

Bloch then briefly pointed out the flimsiness of the prosecution's evidence: the copy of Greenglass's drawings, the copy of the Jell-O box, and the examples of console tables, all of which he argued, had no connection to his client. Bloch then turned to the next task: making the prosecution witnesses look bad.

David Greenglass's action in testifying against his own sister, Bloch asserted, is "repulsive, is revolting, violates every code that any civilization has ever lived by." [39] Bloch also argued that Greenglass convinced the FBI that Julius Rosenberg was a spy in order to save his own skin.

Bloch saved his harshest words, however, for Ruth Greenglass, "who came here all dolled up, arrogant, smart, cute, eager-beaver"; if she "is not the embodiment of evil, I would like to know what person is." [40]

David Greenglass, brother of Ethel Rosenberg, testified against the Rosenbergs at their trial.

Despite his denial that he was asking for sympathy for his clients, Bloch wound up his summation by asking that the jurors identify with the defendants: "If my brother or sister, or if I were sitting in this box, or my child were sitting in that defendant's box, would I convict them on this kind of testimony?" [41]

Alexander Bloch did not present a summation for his client, Ethel Rosenberg. She had chosen to support her husband, and to reach for the jurors' sympathy for her now would have risked turning it against her husband.

Edward Kuntz, Morton Sobell's lead attorney, wasted no time in appealing for sympathy for his client. Since the prosecution's only witness against Morton Sobell had been Max Elitcher, Kuntz chose to discredit his testimony, calling Elitcher a liar and perjurer. Kuntz also argued that the prosecution had attempted to transform his client's innocent trip to Mexico into a flight to avoid arrest. But, when he tried to explain Sobell's use of aliases to get his mail, Kuntz stumbled, unable to make such behavior seem innocent. In closing, the attorney savaged the prosecution, saying that it poisoned the minds of the jury against his client because it had no real evidence against him. Kuntz's attack on Saypol's tactics brought the prosecutor out swinging— and almost brought the trial to an untimely end.

Saypol Sums Up

Irving Saypol was furious at Kuntz's attacks. Never known for his calm temperament, Saypol wanted revenge. Before beginning his summation, he planned to inform the jury that in 1936 Edward Kuntz had been associated with a known left-wing organization. Because of the effect it would have on the jury's opinions about the case, such a comment would have forced the judge to declare a mistrial. Quickly interrupting Saypol, Judge Kaufman stopped him before he could reveal this highly inflammatory information. Years later, Roy Cohn admitted that he had warned Judge Kaufman of Saypol's intentions days before, in time for the judge to silence Saypol. Such communication

Morton Sobell (right), convicted of conspiring to pass secrets of the atomic bomb to the Soviet Union, is transferred to Alcatraz.

between the prosecution and a supposedly impartial judge, however, was itself improper and could well have been grounds for declaring a mistrial, had Kaufman chosen to do so.

Irving Saypol began his summation so convinced of the defendants' guilt and of the gravity of their crimes that he rose to rhetorical heights as yet unmatched in the trial.

> Irving Saypol: Imagine a wheel. In the center of the wheel, Rosenberg, reaching out like the tentacles of an octopus. Rosenberg to David Greenglass. Ethel Rosenberg, Ruth Greenglass; Rosenberg to Harry Gold; Rosenberg, Yakovlev. Information obtained, supplied . . . all the tentacles going to the one center, solely for the one object: the benefit of Soviet Russia. The sources, Government sources, Los Alamos, atomic information; always secret, always classified, always of advantage to a foreign government.[42]

Saypol reminded the jurors that Rosenberg and Sobell had been not only friends but fellow members of the Communist Party for many years. He also argued that their shared history led them to, in his words, worship the Soviet Union and recruit others to commit espionage. Saypol claimed that Julius Rosenberg had intended to become a spy all along. Rosenberg, Saypol said, "had realized the ambition of his life. He had achieved the coveted status of a Communist Party espionage agent."[43]

The prosecutor then went on to reiterate the testimony of Harry Gold, making sure to point out that Gold had testified even though he had nothing to gain, having already been sentenced to a jail term of thirty years for his espionage activities. Gold's only motive in giving testimony, he said, was "the moral satisfaction in his soul."[44] Saypol then directly linked Ethel Rosenberg to the alleged conspiracy.

> Irving Saypol: The atom bomb secrets stolen by Greenglass at the instigation of the Rosenbergs were delivered by Harry Gold right into the hands of an official representative of the Soviet Union. This description of the

atom bomb, destined for delivery to the Soviet Union, was typed up by the defendant Ethel. Just so had she on countless other occasions sat at that typewriter and struck the keys, blow by blow, against her own country in the interests of the Soviets.[45]

Saypol wound up his summation by emphasizing what Manny Bloch had already said, that communism was not the issue; he then turned that argument on its head by saying that, nevertheless, the Rosenbergs' and Sobell's belief in communism motivated them to commit their crimes.

> IRVING SAYPOL: These defendants are not on trial for being Communists. I don't want you to convict them merely because of their Communist activity. Communism, as the testimony has demonstrated, has a very definite place in this case because it is the Communist ideology which teaches worship and devotion to the Soviet Union over our own government. It has provided the motive and inspiration for these people to do the terrible things which have been proven against them.
>
> I am confident that you will render the only verdict possible on the evidence presented before you in this courtroom—that of guilty as charged by the grand jury as to each of these three defendants.[46]

With the end of Saypol's summation, it was time for the jury to decide.

The Jury Decides

After receiving instructions from Judge Kaufman and eating an early dinner, the jury retired to the jury room in the Foley Square courthouse, where, after some initial discussion, a vote was taken. To everyone's surprise, the tally was eleven to one in favor of conviction. The jury was embarrassed at having gotten so close to a consensus so quickly. Because the jury was well aware that the defendants' lives were at stake, they decided to review the evidence and testimony again.

The one holdout, James Gibbons, was a religious man who was reluctant to return a verdict that would mean sentencing Ethel Rosenberg to death. The other jurors pressured him to change his mind but were unsuccessful. They then sent a note to the judge asking about clemency for Ethel. Kaufman, in reply, had the court clerk read his instructions to the jury, which said that they could not consider possible punishments in rendering a verdict. How the defendants might be punished was not relevant in deciding whether or not they were guilty. Since it was already after midnight, a hotel had to be found to put the jury up for the night.

One jurist was reluctant to convict Ethel Rosenberg, especially when that conviction might mean death, because of her role as a mother.

The next morning, deliberations resumed, and the other jurors continued to pressure Gibbons to change his mind. Finally, Gibbons was persuaded by another juror, who asked if he would want Ethel freed to join in another conspiracy that threatened his children.

On March 28, 1951, at about 11 A.M., the jury in the case of *United States of America v. Julius Rosenberg, Ethel Rosenberg, Anatoli A. Yakovlev, also known as "John," David Greenglass and Morton Sobell* reached a verdict: All defendants were found guilty of conspiracy to commit espionage. The verdict was then announced the next day.

Years afterward, three jurors were interviewed about the trial. None had changed their minds about the verdict, despite the worldwide protests and publicity that occurred after the verdict

The Rosenbergs, separated by a heavy wire screen, leave the courthouse after being found guilty of conspiracy to commit espionage.

was announced. They believed David Greenglass and disbelieved his sister. They wondered why Ethel had taken the Fifth Amendment so many times. And, significantly, they had not given much thought to the technical information—until Manny Bloch had moved to clear the courtroom when it was introduced.

The Sentencing

On April 5, 1951, Morton Sobell and the Rosenbergs were brought into a spectator-filled courtroom to hear their fates.

Judge Kaufman's remarks at sentencing reveal the degree to which he was influenced by the political climate of the time.

JUDGE KAUFMAN: I consider your crime worse than murder. Plain deliberate contemplated murder is dwarfed in magnitude by comparison with the crime you have committed. I believe your conduct in putting into the hands of the Russians the A-bomb years before our best scientists predicted Russia would perfect the bomb has already caused, in my opinion, the Communist aggression in Korea, with the resultant casualties exceeding 50,000 and who knows but that millions more of innocent people may pay the price of your treason. Indeed, by your betrayal you undoubtedly have altered the course of history to the disadvantage of our country. In the light of the circumstances, I feel that I must pass such sentence upon the principals in this diabolical conspiracy to destroy a God-fearing nation, which will demonstrate with finality that this nation's security must remain inviolate; that traffic in military secrets, whether promoted by slavish devotion to a foreign ideology or by a desire for monetary gains must cease.

The defendants Julius and Ethel Rosenberg placed their devotion to their cause above their own personal safety. Love for their cause dominated their lives—it was even greater than their love for their children.[47]

Judge Kaufman then pronounced the sentence for Julius and Ethel Rosenberg: that they be put to death in the electric chair.

Kaufman gave Morton Sobell a sentence of thirty years in prison, with the recommendation that he serve his full sentence. The following day, April 6, Judge Kaufman sentenced David

HOOVER'S PLEA FOR MERCY

Two days before Kaufman was scheduled to pass sentence, FBI chief Hoover discussed with Assistant Attorney General Peyton Ford the prospect of death sentences for the Rosenbergs and Sobell. Ford had misgivings about sentencing Ethel Rosenberg to death, and he hoped that the FBI director would, too. Hoover told Ford that he shared Ford's feelings, but from a practical standpoint: He saw that, although a death sentence for Ethel might be approved in the country in that time, in a few years, the public might perceive a death sentence for a mother of two children as inhumane. Moreover, as Radosh and Milton point out in their book *The Rosenberg File*, Hoover reflected the FBI's view that Ethel Rosenberg was just an accomplice of her husband and not the mastermind reported in some news accounts.

Judge Kaufman, who sentenced the Rosenbergs to death, waited several days after the trial to announce the couple's fate, although evidence suggests that he had planned for some time to impose the death penalty.

Greenglass—who had already pled guilty to espionage charges—to fifteen years in prison.

Judge Kaufman waited several days after the trial ended before announcing the fate of the defendants. But evidence suggests that his mind had been made up for some time regarding the sentences he would impose.

Documents from FBI and AEC files indicate that in February 1950, a month before the trial even began, Kaufman had discussed the case with an official in the Justice Department, James McInerny. McInerny told an unnamed AEC official that he had "talked to the judge, and he is prepared to impose [the death penalty] if the evidence warrants." [48]

An FBI document indicates that on March 16, FBI officials knew that Kaufman had informed others that he was prepared to impose the death penalty on the Rosenbergs and Sobell.

Chapter 6

After the Trial

THE ROSENBERGS' PLIGHT FOLLOWING their conviction and sentencing generated little outrage that spring and summer of 1951. It was not until August, when the *National Guardian*, a left-leaning newspaper, printed articles poking holes in the prosecution's case that some people began to question not only the harsh sentences handed the Rosenbergs, but the verdict itself. Some people looked at Judge Kaufman's biased behavior during the trial and at the suspect testimony of the prosecution witnesses, and began to suspect that the Rosenbergs had been framed.

In response to growing doubts among the public, the National Committee to Secure Justice in the Rosenberg Case (known simply as the Rosenberg Committee) was formed in November 1951. The group attracted support not only from those who believed the Rosenbergs were innocent but also from many who felt that, guilty or innocent, the defendants had not received a fair trial. Members of the committee were determined to make people in America and elsewhere aware of the injustice of the verdict, in hopes that a massive expression of public outrage would force the government to hold a new trial.

The committee began its calls for a new trial based on claims of prosecutorial and judicial misconduct that had recently surfaced. But the committee had little money and struggled along for almost a year without rousing the necessary outcry. Then, in the fall of 1952, members of the Communist Party joined the committee in great numbers, and its influence grew.

At that point, the committee changed its demands from holding a new trial to calling for Julius and Ethel Rosenberg's

⚖️ COMMUNISTS IN THE ROSENBERG DEFENSE

People have suggested that the Communist Party became involved in the National Committee to Secure Justice in the Rosenberg Case not out of any desire to help the Rosenbergs, but as part of a cynical attempt to manipulate public opinion and paint a negative picture of the U.S. government. Recently translated Soviet communiqués reveal a concerted effort to shape and mold American public opinion beginning immediately after the verdict, in April 1951, and continuing up till the execution.

The committee was barely surviving during most of 1952, until November, when suddenly money and new volunteers came flooding in. The new members changed the committee. It became much more closed and secretive, and some of its original members resigned in disgust. All efforts to form a broad-based movement of people holding a wide range of political beliefs were stymied. The message of the committee changed as well: It ceased calling for a new trial and began making demands that the Rosenbergs be freed.

freedom. The committee argued that the Rosenbergs were innocent victims of an anti-Communist witch hunt and that they were being railroaded because of America's rampant anti-Semitism—despite the fact that both the judge and the prosecutor in the trial were Jewish. Meanwhile, the legal maneuvering in the case continued.

As legal appeals and petitions for new trials were denied, the committee actually grew in size. To some on the Rosenberg Committee, the denials only proved their contention that a government conspiracy to deny the Rosenbergs justice existed. In an attempt to win public sympathy for the Rosenbergs, the committee published Julius's and Ethel's prison letters.

Public sympathy for the convicted spies grew. Famed physicists Albert Einstein and Harold Urey signed a petition for clemency. Caravans of supporters made their way to Ossining, New York, the site of Sing Sing Prison, to march and sing in support of the imprisoned Rosenbergs. Picketers ringed the White House. The governments of France, Great Britain, and Italy made appeals to the United States to spare the Rosenbergs. Even Pope Pius XII asked for mercy. The pressure on the U.S. government was intense. But neither external pressure nor legal maneuverings could do more than slow the approach of the execution of the Rosenbergs.

Appealing the Verdict: In the Court

After the verdict, Manny Bloch had become a man with one mission: saving the Rosenbergs. Not only was he in charge of the endless legal appeals, writs, and petitions, and was the liaison with the Rosenberg Committee, but he was also the primary caregiver for Michael and Robert, the couple's children.

The first appeal, prepared by Bloch and his associate Gloria Agrin, was filed in the U.S. Court of Appeals, Second Circuit, in January 1952. In it, the attorneys argued three main points: that the government had failed to prove that the Rosenbergs had acted with intent to harm the interests of the United States; that

Demonstrators stand outside the White House in January 1953, protesting the planned execution of the convicted couple.

the testimony of witnesses who hoped to gain leniency in return was by its very nature suspect; and that the interference of Judge Kaufman had prejudiced the jury.

On February 25, 1952, the court denied the appeal on every ground, although one member of the panel, Justice Jerome Frank, indicated that he would have changed the sentence from death to a prison term had it been a legal option available to him.

Next, Bloch filed a petition, called a petition of certiorari, asking the Supreme Court of the United States to review the case. The Court declined to review the case, although several justices expressed some sympathy with the points made in the petition, and a few of them felt that the Rosenbergs' sentence was too harsh.

Despite despair and disappointment from many Rosenberg Committee members, the Communists, who by now were running the committee, saw the Supreme Court's decision as more proof of the corruption of American justice. After the Supreme Court's decision, Judge Kaufman set a new execution date, for January 12, 1953.

Soon afterward, Bloch delivered a second appeal to the court of appeals based on new issues: that Irving Saypol's comments in court had prejudiced the jury and that Ben Schneider, the photographer, had committed perjury when he testified that he had not seen the Rosenbergs since he took their photographs. This appeal was denied as well. The court responded that Bloch should have complained about the prosecutor's conduct when it occurred and that the photographer had only misspoken, with no intent to deceive. A direct appeal to then-president Dwight Eisenhower, in February 1953, was also rejected.

Then in April 1953, a reporter for the left-wing newspaper the *National Guardian* located the missing console table in the house of Julius's mother, Sophie Rosenberg. She was unable to read English and had no idea that she had been harboring such an important piece of evidence.

That same month, a French newspaper published confidential memos that had mysteriously disappeared from the offices of John Rogge, David Greenglass's attorney. These memos cast doubt on the reliability of his client's testimony.

On the basis of these two events, Rosenberg supporters pressed for yet another appeal, but Bloch was hesitant. Believers in the Rosenbergs' innocence were sure that the stolen files represented the tip of an iceberg and that an all-out examination of the Greenglasses' relationship with the government would reveal a conspiracy to frame the Rosenbergs.

In a move that outraged Rosenberg supporters, Manny Bloch ignored calls for him to appeal based on this new evidence. Why Bloch refused to move on this front is uncertain. Authors Radosh and Milton suggest that Bloch might have resisted the notion because he feared that a full disclosure of David Greenglass's statements might have strengthened, rather than weakened the government's case.

But pressure from the committee and elsewhere increased, and Bloch finally relented, drawing up a motion for a new trial based on the discovery of the table and the files. By now, the date of execution had been postponed again, until June 18. Judge Kaufman responded to Bloch's motion by denying it fifteen minutes after it was presented to him.

The Final Act

On June 15, in Washington, D.C., the Supreme Court, by a vote of 5 to 4, denied Bloch's final petition for a stay of execution. The justices then adjourned, preparing to leave on their summer vacations. Only Justice William O. Douglas remained in his chambers, listening to the desperate pleas from the Rosenberg legal team.

On that same afternoon, in New York City, Fyke Farmer, a Tennessee lawyer, joined with Los Angeles attorney David Marshall to ask Judge Kaufman for a stay of execution in the Rosenberg case. Both men represented Irwin Edelman, a Los Angeles political activist and member of the Rosenberg Committee who had written a pamphlet critical of both the defense and prosecution in the Rosenberg trial.

Farmer was persuaded by Edelman's argument that Bloch erred in having the Greenglass sketches and notes kept secret. And he added an argument of his own: The Espionage Act of

On June 15, 1953, the Supreme Court rejected the appeal to spare the lives of Julius and Ethel Rosenberg.

1917, the law under which the Rosenbergs had been tried, did not apply to the crimes they committed. The Atomic Energy Act of 1946, he argued, superseded the earlier law. This specifically excluded the death penalty as a sentencing option unless the defendants intended to harm the national security of the United States, and then it was applied only at the recommendation of the jury.

Kaufman, noting that neither the attorneys nor the petitioner had any connection to the case, denied the petition. But Farmer did not give up. He and Marshall went to Washington to seek a stay of execution from Justice Douglas. After some difficulty gaining the support of Bloch and the legal team in this

"I'LL TAKE CARE OF MY ENEMIES, SAVE ME FROM MY FRIENDS"

No part of the posttrial maneuverings and pleas provides more drama than the Farmer-Edelman brief. Fyke Farmer, who seemed to many to be a simple country lawyer, was actually a smart and able attorney with many connections in the peace movement and civil liberties groups.

Farmer entered into the Rosenberg case when he observed that the Rosenberg Committee was no longer interested in a new trial and it seemed that the Rosenberg attorneys were faltering in their efforts. Although he began by insisting that he wanted to work with Manny Bloch, the negative reaction Farmer received from Bloch and the defense team, and the constant barriers they threw up to his involvement, made Farmer think that the Rosenberg defense was not as interested in defending the Rosenbergs as it was in protecting other interests—perhaps those of the Communist Party.

Fyke Farmer, a small town lawyer, entered the case at the last minute, trying to get a stay of execution and a new trial for the Rosenbergs.

effort, they succeeded in joining forces and presented their petition to Douglas.

On June 17, Supreme Court Justice William O. Douglas granted a stay of execution.

On June 18 the full Supreme Court convened to hear the arguments from Bloch and Farmer, but to no avail: The Court decided to let the execution proceed. It was first scheduled for Friday, June 19, 1953, at 11 P.M., then moved forward to 8:00, to avoid putting the Rosenbergs to death during the Jewish Sabbath, which would begin at sundown.

The End . . . and a Beginning

As a quiet crowd gathered at the gates of Sing Sing, inside Julius Rosenberg's cell on death row, jailers shaved spots on the prisoner's legs in order to attach the electrodes. Earlier that day, Julius had written his will, naming Bloch as guardian of his children. Ethel wrote a last letter and sang quietly to herself.

The Rosenberg defense team poses for photographers on June 19, 1953, the night of the execution.

At a few minutes before eight, Julius, looking pale and shaky, stepped into the white-walled execution chamber. He was strapped into the chair. The warden gave the signal, and the executioner pulled the lever that delivered a killing voltage to the condemned man. Julius Rosenberg was pronounced dead at 8:06 P.M.

Ethel Rosenberg followed her husband's footsteps to the electric chair. Observers noted that, in contrast to her husband, she seemed serene and composed. It took five shocks of electricity before the doctor in attendance checked her pulse and pronounced her dead. In a nearby room, a team of FBI interrogators, who had been waiting for either of the Rosenbergs to break down and confess, packed up their notebooks and recording equipment and left.

In New York's Union Square, a crowd of six thousand listened to the news over an amplified radio broadcast, then dispersed quietly. But in most American cities, there was elation over the executions. In Los Angeles, for example, Irwin Edelman harangued a crowd of people celebrating the Rosenbergs' executions. The crowd did not care to listen to Edelman; some even threatened him with a beating.

Much of the world's reaction was against the United States. Just before the executions, a huge crowd of Rosenberg supporters marched on the American embassy in Paris. The crowd turned into a mob that battled with police. Hundreds were arrested, and one man was killed. In Rome, graffiti appeared overnight calling for "Death To the Killers of the Rosenbergs."[49]

Manny Bloch spent the rest of his life in the grip of the Rosenberg case. His obsession with the trial and its aftermath had destroyed his marriage. His newly acquired notoriety as a defender of "atom spies" kept prospective clients away, and his law practice dwindled to almost nothing. And the New York Bar Association began looking into disbarring him because of a statement he had made when the Supreme Court vacated Justice Douglas's stay of execution: "I am ashamed to be an American."[50]

Nevertheless, Bloch did his duty. He found a couple, Abel and Anne Meeropol, willing to adopt the Rosenberg children, Michael and Robert. He also oversaw the trust fund that had been established for their care. In January 1954, Bloch's associate, Gloria Agrin, went to check on her employer when he failed to show up at the office. She found him dead of a heart attack.

The other defendants in the case fared better. David Greenglass served his fifteen-year sentence and led a quiet life with Ruth and their children after he was released. Morton Sobell served his thirty-year sentence and became an author and lecturer upon his release.

Accompanied by their grandmother, the Rosenbergs' two sons, Michael and Robert, watch as Rabbi Abraham Kronbac offers a prayer for their parents.

Later Evidence and the Verdict of History

For many people today, the issue of the Rosenbergs' guilt and their harsh fate is still very much a blot on America's history. But new information has recently been revealed that strongly suggests that questions about their guilt may be laid to rest.

Documents from a top-secret intelligence effort called the Venona Project, released only in 1995, point unambiguously to Julius Rosenberg's complicity in espionage.

On February 1, 1943, the U.S. Army's Signal Intelligence Service, a forerunner of the National Security Agency, began a small, very secret program, code-named VENONA, that intercepted and decoded Soviet diplomatic messages. These intercepts mentioned dozens, probably hundreds, of KGB agents operating in the United States.

Although the KGB clerks were careful to use coded names such as "Good Girl" and "Antenna" for their agents (called "assets"), once in a while they slipped up. In an astonishing example of carelessness, a November 27, 1944, KGB message mentions "ETHEL, 29 years old, married five years—a FELLOWCOUN-TRYMAN [code word for Communist Party member] since 1938." The message said she "knows about her husband's work," but was in "delicate health" and "does not work."[51] Later intercepts identified "Ethel's" husband by his code name "Liberal."

According to the handful of decoded Venona intercepts, agents who were far more productive than the Rosenbergs remain to this day unidentified and unpunished. For example, someone named "Robert" is mentioned in dozens of cables between 1943 and 1948. One time he sent his Soviet contacts no less than fifty-six rolls of film of classified U.S. sites and other information. "Robert" has never been unmasked.

The Rosenberg children, Michael and Robert Meeropol, have always maintained that their parents were innocent. After the release of the Venona documents, in July 1995, they issued this statement:

Nothing in the 49 VENONA documents released by the National Security Agency and the CIA on July 11 cause us to alter our positions that:

1. our parents Ethel and Julius Rosenberg were not guilty as charged;
2. their conviction was based upon perjured testimony and fabricated evidence;
3. that government agents and agencies orchestrated our parents' frame-up which resulted in their execution.[52]

With the Venona documents in hand, it is clear that those who argued that the government was manipulating public opinion with its tales of the "Communist spy rings" operating in the United States were wrong. With the United States the declared winner in the now-ended cold war, it all seems moot, but the fears of those at the time were very real.

A second piece of evidence came to light in 1997, when a former Soviet KGB agent named Aleksandr Feklisov came to the United States for a visit. In an interview with reporter Michael Dobbs in the *Washington Post*, Feklisov said he met with

THE VENONA CABLES: CRACKING THE KGB CODE

The Soviet codes in the transmissions intercepted by the U.S. government's analysts were extremely complex, and it was not until 1945 that the Venona team was able to begin to decrypt the first Soviet diplomatic cables. Using information gained from an FBI interrogation of Igor Gouzenko, a Soviet military intelligence clerk who defected to Canada, and other information from former Communists Elizabeth Bentley and Whitaker Chambers in 1945 gave the cryptanalysts key character sets they needed to crack the codes.

In the summer of 1946, cryptographer Meredith Gardner was finally able to decode a handful of KGB code character sets, allowing parts of cables moving between New York and Moscow to be read for the first time.

Gardner then turned his attention to decoding the more than two thousand coded cables intercepted since 1943. The first cable he decoded listed the names of the leading A-bomb scientists who, at the time, had been locked behind the walls of the Los Alamos site.

Not long after that, Gardner translated the first of the Rosenberg cables. In all, Julius Rosenberg is referred to (by his code name) in twenty of the forty-nine decoded cables that have been declassified by the National Security Agency.

Julius Rosenberg more than fifty times from 1943 to 1946, and he credited him with helping to organize an important industrial espionage ring and with handing over top-secret information on military electronics.

Feklisov insisted that Ethel Rosenberg never had any direct contact with Soviet intelligence, but he believed that she was probably aware of her husband's activities. More important, neither Rosenberg offered any "useful information" about the atom bomb, the crime for which they were executed. "My morality does not allow me to keep silent," said Feklisov, who claimed he is the only Soviet intelligence officer still alive with intimate personal knowledge of the Rosenberg case. "Julius was a great sympathizer of the Soviet Union. There were others who also believed in communism, but were unwilling to fight. Julius was a true revolutionary, who was willing to sacrifice himself for his beliefs." [53]

What Julius Rosenberg did give to the Soviets, according to Feklisov, were plans and a mockup of a proximity fuse, a detonator used in anti-aircraft shells that can explode by just getting within a certain range of its target. The fuse was a closely guarded military secret, and its production at the Emerson Radio Factory, where Rosenberg worked, was tightly supervised. Feklisov said that Rosenberg painstakingly assembled a duplicate fuse out of discarded spare parts and then smuggled the device out of the factory, announcing proudly: "I have a Christmas present for the Red Army." [54]

Even the most ardent believers in the Rosenbergs' complete innocence have a hard time with the Feklisov interview. Indeed, recent documents uncovered in KGB files in Moscow tend to support Feklisov's claim that Rosenberg was an active spy for the Soviets.

Conclusion

The new information revealed by the recently declassified Venona documents and the statements of some of those involved make it clear that Julius Rosenberg was actively engaged in spying for the Soviet Union. It has also become clear, however, that

On June 21, 1953, the Rosenbergs were laid to rest in Farmingdale, New York, with a crowd of mourners in attendance.

not as much damage was done to America's national security as has been argued by the most strident defenders of the Rosenbergs' execution.

The case against Ethel Rosenberg is demonstrably weaker than the one against her husband, although it seems unlikely that she was not aware of Julius's activities. But given both the statements of Feklisov and the decoded Venona documents, she was probably not directly involved. In light of her lack of direct involvement, the death penalty for Ethel Rosenberg seems unwarranted.

Aside from lingering questions regarding the Rosenbergs' guilt, there still remains the fact that the United States and the Soviet Union were not at war when these crimes were committed. Legal scholars have argued convincingly that even the harsher espionage statute was never intended to allow the execution of those who spied for America's allies. Even with an amendment to the espionage statute known as the "Rosenberg law," which was passed in 1954 and permitted the death sentence for individuals who engaged in peacetime espionage, no one convicted of espionage since the Rosenbergs has been sentenced to death.

Given the fear of communism that overtook the United States in the 1950s, it is questionable whether there could have been another outcome. The enduring lessons of the Rosenberg trial and its aftermath are twofold: that, whatever cause was served by the execution of Julius and Ethel Rosenberg, their deaths remain a blemish on American society, and that, when a nation is swept by paranoia, the innocent suffer along with the guilty.

Notes

Chapter 1: The Pursuit of the Rosenbergs

1. Quoted in Ronald Radosh and Joyce Milton, *The Rosenberg File: A Search for the Truth*. New York: Holt, Rinehart, and Winston, 1983, p. 14.
2. Quoted in Oliver Pilat, *The Atom Spies*. New York: Charles Scribner's Sons, 1952, p. 183.
3. Quoted in Radosh and Milton, *The Rosenberg File*, p. 39.
4. Quoted in Radosh and Milton, *The Rosenberg File*, p. 43.
5. Quoted in Radosh and Milton, *The Rosenberg File*, p. 56.
6. Trial Transcript, *United States of America v. Julius Rosenberg, Ethel Rosenberg, Anatoli A. Yakovlev, also known as "John", David Greenglass and Morton Sobell,* U.S. District Court, Southern District of New York, C. 134–135, pp. 1, 137.
7. Quoted in Radosh and Milton, *The Rosenberg File*, p. 99.
8. Trial Transcript, p. 2.

Chapter 2: The Prelude to Trial

9. Trial Transcript, p. 173.
10. Trial Transcript, p. 1,535.

Chapter 3: The Trial Begins

11. Quoted in Radosh and Milton, *The Rosenberg File*, p. 171.
12. Trial Transcript, p. 180.
13. Trial Transcript, p. 180.
14. Trial Transcript, p. 930.
15. Trial Transcript, p. 499.
16. Trial Transcript, p. 502.
17. Trial Transcript, p. 692.
18. Trial Transcript, p. 700.
19. Trial Transcript, p. 707.
20. Trial Transcript, p. 728.
21. Trial Transcript, p. 728.
22. Trial Transcript, p. 822.
23. Trial Transcript, p. 829.

Chapter 4: The Defense's Turn

24. Quoted in Radosh and Milton, *The Rosenberg File*, p. 191.
25. Quoted in Douglas T. Miller and Marion Nowak, *The Fifties: The Way We Really Were*. Garden City, NY: Doubleday, 1977, p. 22.
26. Trial Transcript, p. 1,065.
27. Trial Transcript, p. 1,080.
28. Trial Transcript, p. 1,078.
29. Trial Transcript, pp. 1,277–78.
30. Trial Transcript, p. 1,303.
31. Trial Transcript, pp. 1,324–26.
32. Trial Transcript, pp. 1,317–18.
33. Radosh and Milton, *The Rosenberg File*, p. 260.
34. Trial Transcript, pp. 1,370–71.
35. Trial Transcript, p. 1,396.
36. Trial Transcript, pp. 1,428–29.

Chapter 5: The Battle for Life

37. Trial Transcript, pp. 1,452, 1,453.
38. Trial Transcript, p. 1,454.
39. Trial Transcript, p. 1,467.
40. Trial Transcript, pp. 1,476, 1,477.
41. Trial Transcript, p. 1,492.
42. Trial Transcript, pp. 1513–14.
43. Trial Transcript, p. 1,516.
44. Trial Transcript, p. 1,521.
45. Trial Transcript, p. 1,523.
46. Trial Transcript, p. 1,536.
47. Trial Transcript, pp. 1,614–16.
48. Quoted in Radosh and Milton, *The Rosenberg File*, p. 277.

Chapter 6: After the Trial

49. Quoted in Radosh and Milton, *The Rosenberg File*, p. 419.
50. Quoted in Robert and Michael Meeropol, *We Are Your Sons: The Legacy of Ethel and Julius Rosenberg*. Boston: Houghton Mifflin, 1975, p. 244.
51. National Security Agency, "Venona Documents" (photo reproduction), Washington, DC, November 27, 1944. www.

nsa.gov:8080/docs/venona/docs/Nov44/27_Nov_1944_R1.gif.

52. Michael Meeropol and Robert Meeropol, "Released Venona Documents Demonstrate Government Duplicity," July 17, 1995. www.english.upenn.edu/~afilreis/50s/meeropol–on–rosenbergs.html.

53. Michael Dobbs, "Julius Rosenberg Spied, Russian Says," *Washington Post*, March 16, 1997.

54. Dobbs, "Julius Rosenberg Spied, Russian Says."

Timeline

July 1949
Government cryptographers decipher a KGB document that contains a report written by Klaus Fuchs.

January 24, 1950
Klaus Fuchs, questioned by MI-6, confesses to espionage, naming an American, "Raymond," as his contact.

May 22, 1950
Fuchs shown photos of Gold. Unable to positively identify him as "Raymond."

June 15, 1950
Gold identifies a photo of Greenglass' Albuquerque residence as the place he picked up secret documents, FBI calls David Greenglass in for questioning; Greenglass names Julius Rosenberg as the man who recruited him into the spy ring.

June 16, 1950
Julius Rosenberg is called in for questioning by the FBI; he hires Manny Bloch as his attorney.

June 24, 1950
Morton Sobell flees to Mexico.

July 15, 1950
Julius Rosenberg is arrested on charge of conspiracy to commit espionage.

July 27–August 9, 1950
Al Sarant and his girlfriend lose their FBI tail and vanish in Mexico.

August 11, 1950
Ethel Rosenberg is arrested on the same conspiracy charge as her husband.

August 17, 1950
Morton Sobell is forcibly deported from Mexico and arrested by the FBI.

March 6, 1951
The trial of the Rosenbergs and Sobell begins.

March 28, 1951
The Rosenberg trial ends and goes to the jury.

March 29, 1951
The jury returns with a guilty verdict for the Rosenbergs and Sobell.

April 5, 1951
Judge Kaufman sentences the Rosenbergs to death and Sobell to thirty years in prison.

April 6, 1951
Bloch files an appeal for the Rosenbergs.

February 25, 1952
Judge Kaufman denies appeal.

October 13, 1952
Rosenberg attorneys appeal to Supreme Court for certiorari.

November 7, 1952
Judge Kaufman sets new execution date as January 12, 1953.

December 3, 1952
Appeals court stays execution of the Rosenbergs.

December 30, 1952
Judge Kaufman refuses appeal and sets March 9, 1953, as the new date for execution.

January 14, 1953
Bloch files appeal with appeals court, which grants stay of execution.

May 25, 1953
Supreme Court denies appeal; new execution date is set for June 18, 1953.

June 6–12, 1953
Console table is found; Bloch files appeal based on new evidence; Judge Kaufman denies appeal; Bloch appeals to the Supreme Court.

June 15, 1953
Supreme Court denies appeal on a 5 to 4 vote.

June 19, 1953
Julius and Ethel Rosenberg are executed in the electric chair at Sing Sing Prison.

For Further Reading

Thomas S. Arms, *Encyclopedia of the Cold War*. New York: Facts On File, 1994. An encyclopedia on the era containing topics from "Arms Race" to "Zirinovsky."

"Decades of Cold War," *The American Heritage Illustrated History of the United States*, vol. 16. Englewood Cliffs, NJ: Silver-Burdett, 1989. A chronology of events.

William Dudley, ed., *The Cold War: Opposing Viewpoints*. San Diego: Greenhaven Press, 1992. Collection of articles on all aspects of the Cold War.

Robert Goldston, *The Coming of the Cold War*. New York: Macmillan, 1973. A look at the countries and forces involved in the origins of the Cold War.

Derek Heater, *Witness to History Series: The Cold War*. New York: Bookwright Press, 1989. The cold war in the words of its participants.

Morrie Helitzer, *The Cold War*. New York: Franklin Watts, 1977. A look at American and Russian attitudes from the end of World War II to Vietnam and détente.

Thomas G. Peterson, *Meeting the Cold War Threat: Truman to Reagan*. New York: Oxford University Press, 1988. Shows how American presidents confronted communism.

Works Consulted

Paul Boyer, *By the Bomb's Early Light: American Thought and Culture at the Dawn of the Atomic Age.* Chapel Hill: University of North Carolina Press, 1985. An examination of American behavior in the years after the atomic bomb.

Michael Dobbs, "Julius Rosenberg Spied, Russian Says," *Washington Post*, March 16, 1997. An extensive interview with spymaster Feklisov.

Robert and Michael Meeropol, *We Are Your Sons: The Legacy of Ethel and Julius Rosenberg.* Boston: Houghton Mifflin, 1975. Biography and apologia by the sons of Ethel and Julius Rosenberg.

Douglas T. Miller and Marion Nowak, *The Fifties: The Way We Really Were.* Garden City, NY: Doubleday, 1977. An extensive cultural and political overview of the period.

Louis Nizer, *The Implosion Conspiracy.* Garden City, NY: Doubleday, 1973. A pro-prosecution view of the Rosenberg trial.

William O'Neill, *American High: The Years of Confidence, 1945–1960.* New York: Free Press, 1986. A look at American popular culture and politics in the postwar era.

David M. Oshinsky, *A Conspiracy So Immense: The World of Joe McCarthy.* New York: Free Press, 1983. A biography of the senator from Wisconsin.

Oliver Pilat, *The Atom Spies.* New York: Charles Scribner's Sons, 1952. Anti-Communist tract by a journalist close to the Rosenberg prosecutor.

Ronald Radosh and Joyce Milton, *The Rosenberg File: A Search for the Truth.* New York: Holt, Rinehart and Winston, 1983. The most recent and thorough examination of the trial and its aftermath.

Walter and Miriam Schneir, *Invitation to an Inquest.* Garden City, NY: Doubleday, 1965. Argues that the Rosenbergs' attorney did not present a good case and that no spy ring existed.

Joseph Sharlitt, *Fatal Error: The Miscarriage of Justice That Sealed the Rosenbergs' Fate.* New York: Charles Scribner's Sons, 1988.

This book makes a convincing argument that prosecutorial misconduct and legal errors doomed the Rosenbergs.

Malcolm Sharp, *Was Justice Done? The Rosenberg-Sobell Case.* New York: Monthly Review Press, 1956. The attorney who helped Bloch prepare the first appeal brief examines flaws in the prosecution's case.

Morton Sobell, *On Doing Time.* New York: Charles Scribner's Sons, 1974. Sobell's autobiography, mostly about his life in prison.

Kaufman Papers (informational pamphlet). National Committee to Secure Justice for the Rosenbergs, Chicago, 1975. Presents new information on the Rosenberg judge's ex parte conversations with the FBI and prosecutors.

Trial Transcript, *United States of America v. Julius Rosenberg, Ethel Rosenberg, Anatoli A. Yakovlev, also known as "John", David Greenglass and Morton Sobell,* U.S. District Court, Southern District of New York, C. 134–135, 1951. The official trial transcript.

University of Missouri, "Famous Trials" Project. www.law.umkc.edu/faculty/projects/ftrials/rosenb/ROSENB.htm. Website with much information and photographs on the Rosenberg case.

John Wexley, *The Judgment of Julius and Ethel Rosenberg.* New York: Cameron & Kahn, 1955. The first book to argue the Rosenbergs' innocence.

Stephen J. Whitfield, *The Culture of the Cold War.* Baltimore: Johns Hopkins University Press, 1991. A recent overview of television, film, the press, and religion in the postwar era.

Index

Picture Credits

About the Author

Francis Moss is a television writer and book author. He has written over a hundred episodes of various children's television shows such as *Spider-Man*, *X-Men*, and *CatDog*. His two books, *Internet for Kids* and *Make Your Own Web Page*, are very popular. A third book, *How to Find Things on the Web*, is due out next year. Francis also designs web sites for many businesses and individuals. He lives in Los Angeles, California, with his wife and daughter. His son works on computers for the U.S. Army.